Mind Your Own Business

SECOND EDITION

The Complete Guide to Profitable Powersports Dealerships

John Wyckoff

Windsor Media Enterprises, LLC
Rochester, New York

MYOB-2

Mind Your Own Business, Second Edition

The Complete Guide to Profitable Powersports Dealerships

by John Wyckoff

ISBN: 0-9765304-0-6

Project Editor: Anita Campbell
Cover Design
& Page Layout: Tom Collins

Published by
Windsor Media Enterprises, LLC
Rochester, New York
USA

Available online at: www.WindsorMediaEnterprises.com
as well as other booksellers and distributors worldwide.
For information on bulk orders and discounts,
please contact:

Speical Orders
Windsor Media Enterprises, LLC
620 Park Avenue #317
Rochester, NY 14607

info@WindsorMediaEnterprises.com

CONTENTS

FOREWORD

Welcome to the completely updated Second Edition of my book, **Mind Your Own Business**.

MYOB - 2 contains over 100 pages of additional insights developed in the two decades since the original book was published.

The Second Edition has been updated to reflect the many changes in the industry over the past 20 years. Those changes include the increasing sophistication of dealerships.

The Second Edition also covers the growth of dealerships into what is now known as the powersports industry – beyond motorcycles, to categories including ATVs and watercraft.

It reflects changes in the way products are sold, including the influence of the Internet. It also reflects the greater knowledge today's consumers have relating to the products, dealerships and P&A retailers.

Why I wrote this book

Throughout my 40-year career I've been studying and researching merchandising and marketing as it relates to recreational products. My main concern was how it pertains to the retail powersports business.

My travels have given me the opportunity to spend countless hours with many wonderful dealers around the world. Dealers who, collectively, know more about the business than any one person ever will. Many were kind enough to share some of their ideas with me. Those ideas have been corroborated and are incorporated in this book.

For the past two decades I've been conducting seminars and working with importers, manufacturers, warehouse distributors, dealers and their sales staffs. During the same time I've written marketing articles for trade and consumer motorcycle and powersports publications.

I wrote the original edition of the book because I'd been asked by some of those attending my seminars if the information we covered was available in book form. It wasn't. I referred them to a particular trade publication in hopes they could find what they were looking for. Sometimes I'd send them copies of articles from my library.

Eventually I wrote the book

The original edition has been out of print now for many years. Yet I continued to get requests for my book. That's why I created this Second Edition, **MYOB - 2**.

More new people are entering the powersports industry every day. Most are coming in with very little training. Few have any sense of the history of our industry. Given the changing nature of the industry, including the influence of new entrants and new products, there is little chance these new people will be able to get the help, training and information they need to be successful.

The powersports business has been good to me. I'm a motorcyclist and like both the business, and the people in it. I know of no other industry where all the players know each other by first name. This industry is more like an extended family.

I've enjoyed riding my motorcycles and spending time with many of the riders I've met over the years. It is my honest belief that if more people rode motorcycles, there would be less crime and violence in the world. Motorcycle riding is a natural high.

Although I'm called an optimist (among other things), I believe I can have a positive impact on the industry by helping the people who work for the dealerships. When they become more professional, they'll introduce more people into the wonderful world of motorcycling and powersports. If more motorcycles and powersports units are sold, regardless of brand, our industry and the rest of humanity – I'd like to believe – will benefit.

Lest I lead you astray, the information in this book did not come through divine wisdom. I have to thank literally hundreds, perhaps even thousands of people who have helped guide me for the past 40-odd years.

NOTE: The following is addressed to feminists, sexists, linguists, grammarians and those concerned with gender-specific pronouns and adjectives.

Motorcycling and the world of powersports traditionally was a male-dominated sport. In recent years many more women have become involved – a fact for which I'm grateful. However, I find it cumbersome and awkward to use "her/him," "herself/himself," "he/she," and "he or she." Therefore, I will use only the male gender to define customers, dealers, etc. You may translate the gender to suit yourself. If you find it impossible to do so, forgive me. I just couldn't face the clumsiness and was unable find a reasonable alternative; such are the limitations of the English language or of this author.

John Wyckoff
Corrales, New Mexico
January 2005

Chapter 1

EVALUATE YOUR STORE

If everything seems to be going OK, why would you take the time and effort to evaluate your store? The simple answer is: You need a report card to see just how well you're really doing.

If you evaluate your store based on criteria you establish will the results be meaningful? I doubt it. That would be like filling out your own report card in school. While you might like the result the facts wouldn't have changed. Maybe you gave yourself an "A" in geography but you still can't find Afghanistan on a map.

It's a fact that soon after you learn something you start to forget it.

Research has shown that the average college graduate remembers less than two percent of what he was taught – no, not ten years later but within the first two years. We seldom remember why we once did something; just that we did it. For example: Once you had everything in the store exactly the way you thought it should be; now the walls need repainting and the signs are faded. Perhaps you've forgotten why you had the store neat and clean but now have let it deteriorate.

From time to time everyone needs to step back and take a look at what they are doing and have done, and why. Because there's nothing so constant as change, we must assure ourselves that we're capable of changing too. When we spend most of our waking hours in our stores it's easy for us to overlook problems that evolved without our even noticing them.

I've talked with many dealers who have told me they used to do things differently and displayed with more dynamics, for example. When I ask why they don't do it now, their response is, all too often, "I guess we just got busy and forgot." We're all too busy. However, we must take the time to look more closely at what we're too busy doing. To achieve that, I've prepared a simple fifteen-point report card. Why not take the time now and see how you're actually doing.

Answer the following questions as true (T) or false (F). These are not trick questions. Everything covered here will be discussed in the rationale that follows this simple test. Or where applicable, I'll cover it in later chapters.

More and more dealerships these days have more than one location. If you have multiple locations, take the test for each location separately. Simply photocopy the Store Evaluation page and make multiple copies.

And no, Afghanistan is not next to Saudi Arabia or Iraq, although many assume that's where it is.

STORE EVALUATION

	T	F	
1. I'm open at least six days a week and three evenings	__	__	7
2. My store is always clean and neat	__	__	6
3. My Yellow Pages ad includes my Web address and hours	__	__	4
4. NO smoking, eating or drinking on the showroom floor	__	__	6
5. I have a minimum of two full-length mirrors	__	__	6
6. I carry all common sizes of gloves, tires etc.	__	__	5
7. My store is in a convenient location	__	__	4
8. I have plenty of parking for my customers	__	__	4
9. Everyone on my staff has been adequately trained	__	__	6
10. My customers are greeted within the first 2 minutes	__	__	6
11. My F&I program is comprehensive	__	__	7
12. All employees are appropriately dressed	__	__	6
13. All employees read the trade and retail magazines	__	__	5
14. We always follow up after the sale	__	__	5
15. I have an excellent relationship with my suppliers	__	__	7
16. I have a Web site that is updated weekly	__	__	8
17. My DMS software is less than 3 years old	__	__	8

HOW TO SCORE:

Add the numbers next to each question you marked false: ________

Subtract the total from 100: ________

Your total score is: ________

There is no way to score "0" on this test. In the unlikely event you marked every question false, you would nonetheless have a score of three. If you are still in the powersports retail business then I feel you deserve something. Three seemed like a reasonable number.

If your score was between 80 and 100, you're a very successful dealer and are doing most things right. The chapters, which follow, will serve to help train your future employees and aid you in honing your skills.

If your score was between 70 and 80, you're getting along fine, for now. There are, however, some specific areas you may want to address. There may be several specific chapters that will be more important to you than others.

For those of you who scored 50 to 70, you've no time to lose. Set your priorities and begin to attack you problems now!

Did you score under 50? If so, don't feel too bad; I wrote the test with failure in mind. Unless you're out of your "comfort zone" you'll find it difficult to make changes. If you've been stunned by a low score and don't blame me, you'll begin to make substantive changes in your operation.

You may have wondered about the meaning of the numbers to the right of each statement. They will become clear after you read the following rationale.

RATIONALE FOR STORE EVALUATION

The numbers to the right of each question relate (roughly) to the percentage of sales or profit at jeopardy. These ratings are subjective. I have attempted to quantify the potential impact you may expect. For example: If you marked question number one false, you could anticipate an increase of about seven percent in sales by extending your store hours. Question number eight, about parking, has a lesser consequence. If you answered false, it may represent a possible four percent increase in sales.

Each numbered statement listed in the test is repeated below and is followed by the rationale in an attempt to show that if the statement is true you benefit. If you marked the statement false, my rationale offers you a reasonable argument to change.

1) I'm open at least six days a week and three evenings

If you marked this false, you may be catering to the unemployed. Purchasing a motorcycle is a **major** investment. Few unemployed people purchase high-ticket adult toys. Most of your customers work for a living. Normal work hours are from 8am to 5pm. Unless you're purposely catering to the unemployed, consider adjusting your store hours as a convenience to potential buyers.

That's even more critical today. Today's shoppers have become used to shopping at all hours, from Wal-Marts that stay open 24 hours, to the 24/7 Internet.

Department stores report they do 60 to 80 percent of their business on weekends and during evening hours. Customers have become accustomed to shopping after dinner and on weekends. If you're closed when it's convenient for them to visit you, they'll be forced to go to your competitor.

That competitor may not be another motorcycle, watercraft, or snowmobile dealer. It may be a computer store or truck dealer.

Or the customer will log on to the Internet and shop that way. Or even find a used unit on eBay or one of the online classifieds sites. (We'll cover Internet sales later on.)

Mall hours are generally from 10 in the morning to 9 in the evening during the week, and until 6 in the evening on weekends. Researchers have found these hours best accommodate most buyer's needs. (Malls are discussed at length in a later chapter.)

2) My store is always clean and neat

Shopping malls, big box retailers, and franchised grocery, hardware and drug stores, have set the standard for cleanliness. If your store doesn't meet the customer's expectations for cleanliness, he may experience a level of discomfort that will have a negative impact on his buying attitude.

> Uncomfortable people don't spend money; comfortable people do. A store that isn't clean is distracting and makes people uncomfortable.

3) My Yellow Pages ad includes my Web address and hours

People who regularly shop at your store don't use the Yellow Pages; **NEW** customers do.

More importantly, today's consumer goes to the Web to find information. That said, we still need the Yellow Pages. However, I now recommend that we place smaller ads and do so in more such books not only in our immediate market but also perhaps in adjacent markets.

In the original edition of **Mind Your Own Business**, I suggested that we use large ads filled with information. That was before the Internet. Now I suggest the smallest possible ad with your address, phone number, hours and in big type, Web address. My reasoning relates to recent studies that indicate people use the Yellow Pages to find phone numbers and not much else. Considering how much it costs each month to have an eye-catching ad I believe those dollars could be better spent on your Web site.

> NEW customers are the life blood of any retail business! Make it easy for them by including your Web address and business hours.

Read the chapter on Yellow Pages for a more in-depth discussion of what yours should contain to be as effective as possible. Read the chapter on Web sites to understand how to leverage the Internet for your dealership.

4) NO smoking, eating or drinking on the showroom floor

By now most retail outlets have banned smoking inside their premises, either because of local ordinances which prohibit smoking, or because they are aware that our society seriously frowns upon smoking. Need I say more about not allowing smoking on the showroom floor?

The same rule applies to the consumption of food and drink in the showroom. An employee eating his sandwich or crunching the last of the ice in his supersized soft drink, prevents him from concentrating and getting involved in buying. These activities are very distracting.

Not to mention that eating and drinking distract from the professionalism of the look – and smell – of your dealership.

No employee should be allowed to smoke, eat or drink on the showroom floor.

I suggest you extend this ban to customers in the showroom too. It's the one exception I make to my rule about not telling the customer "NO." Virtually all retail outlets have adopted similar rules, and your customers will not find it unusual.

5) I have a minimum of two full-length mirrors

I'd prefer you have three mirrors arranged in a "U" shape to enable the customer to see himself from the sides and back. However, I'll settle for two. Mirrors allow the customer to get a positive image of himself.

Selling apparel is almost impossible without full-length mirrors. Mirrors also reduce theft, and make stores look larger and better lit.

6) I carry all common sizes of gloves, tires, etc

The main aim of retailing should be to allow the customer instant gratification. When a buyer parts with his money, he wants to walk out with the product; that's instant gratification. Dealers who stock a product line – helmets, leathers, tires – should stock ALL sizes, both common and uncommon.

When the customer is asked to wait while you order the item for him, you have denied him that gratification. Be aware that you are acting as a go-between for a **mail-order** company when you can't instantly provide what the customer wants to purchase.

Research reported in *Boardroom Reports* has concluded that the mail-order business is growing for one basic reason: retailers don't have the merchandise in stock. Price, according to the same research, accounted for only 16 percent of the reason consumers listed as when they buy from mail-order companies.

7) My store is in a convenient location

Someone once said the three most important considerations for a retail store are location, location and location. If your location is not what it should be don't let cost be your only criteria when contemplating a new address.

A high-traffic site means incremental business and growth potential which will more than offset any additional rent or mortgage costs. When more people walk or drive past your store, you may find you have to spend less money in advertising. That's an important thing to consider for those of you working on an already tight budget.

8) I have plenty of parking for my customers

If you have limited parking, insist that the employees park in a remote location. The prime parking spaces should be available for your customers. You and your employees earn your living from customer's purchases. Make life easy for your customers by keeping the close-in parking spaces open for them.

9) Everyone on my staff has been adequately trained

Trained employees know what's expected of them. Professionalism is an attitude fostered by training. Fewer mistakes are a benefit of training. Training should be an on-going and important component of every department of your business.

10) My customers are greeted within the first two minutes

Few things cause as much frustration as being ignored in a store. Think about how you feel when a store employee treats you as though you're invisible. Even if you're busy with a customer, acknowledge anyone who comes through your door. Tell them to make themselves at home and that you'll be with them as soon as possible.

The customer wants to feel he's important. Ignoring him makes him feel unappreciated and unimportant. The expected reaction to being ignored is anger and hostility; a poor beginning to a relationship.

11) My F&I program is comprehensive

Many motorcycles and watercraft have to be sold twice; once by the salesperson and again by whoever has to arrange the financing. An easily understood, comprehensive finance and insurance program simplifies a salesperson's job. It makes it easier for the customer to buy. Best of all, it has the ability to become a substantial profit center.

For the dwindling few of you who don't use computers, now's your chance. A good F&I computer program will pay for itself and the computer more quickly than you can imagine.

12) All employees are appropriately dressed

How can you tell a customer from an employee? It's embarrassing for a customer to ask a question, only to discover he just asked another customer.

It's easy to tell who's who at the doctor's office, at church, at an attorney's office or at a construction job site. Professionals dress according to their vocation; make sure your professional staff dresses to fit the part. Appropriate attire should include a name tag worn by every employee who comes in contact with the consumer. In another chapter, I discuss other attributes of the professional.

13) All employees read the trade and retail magazines

With a few exceptions, dealers receive all the trade magazines and at least a few retail motorcycle magazines. The information in the trade publications, including "how to" articles, could be of immense value to employees. There is no better source of timely information about new products, trends, legislation, management techniques and the competition, than the trade press. It's an embarrassment if the customer knows more about a product than the salesperson. **ALL** trade and retail magazines should be read and important points highlighted by management and circulated to all appropriate employees.

14) We always follow up after the sale

A satisfied customer is the dealer's best salesperson. Follow-up shows you care. The more personal the follow-up, the better. Look for trouble. God doesn't make motorcycles, watercraft or snowmobiles. Imperfect people do. There has never been, nor will there ever be, the perfect motorcycle. Your follow-up should look for problems. Their solutions will bond the customer to **YOUR** dealership. Elsewhere in this book I elaborate on follow-up and give you a step-by-step program designed to get results.

15) I have an excellent relationship with my suppliers

Dealers and OEMs are not, and should not be, adversaries. No OEM in our industry has more than 1,500 customers. Without dealers, the OEM can't sell anything.

> Don't confront, communicate. This also holds true for any other suppliers with whom you trade.

When selecting suppliers, don't let price be your only consideration. Ask for, and expect, help, training and support. Make your relationships with your OEM and warehouse distributor a two-way street. Be open and willing to learn and negotiate without being hostile.

16) I have a Web site that is updated weekly

The growth of online sales has outpaced the growth of store sales by 4-to-1. This means that the Internet is no longer a "nice to have" – it is a necessity. In my visits to dealerships I am amazed by the number of dealers who do not have a Web site.

Consumers today are more comfortable on the Internet. They are used to going to the Web to look for information about a business. They expect to see your store address, an interactive map to the premises, hours of operation, products you carry, and other important information.

Security on the Web has gotten better. People are used to purchasing items and paying by credit card over the Web.

Update your Web site regularly, at least once a week. A Web site that hasn't been updated is useless and a waste of money. If a consumer goes to the home page twice and sees the exact same thing each time, he won't go back.

Try putting a customer's name on your Web site when you update it. Tell customers that they get a free T-shirt if they see their name on your site and call you. You'll have happy customers, it will force you to update your Web site, and it will bring traffic to your site.

Every piece of paper in the office should have your Web address on it: letterhead, business cards, invoices, brochures – **everything**.

17) My DMS software is less than 3 years old

In the old days a dealer could get by without a DMS. Times have changed! Every dealer today must have a Dealer Management System. And any DMS software that hasn't been updated in 3 years is obsolete.

The DMS vendors have made substantial improvements in their software in recent years. The report generators offered by the DMS vendors today are marvelous. They give you the information and visibility you need to run your dealership and make informed decisions. If you are still using old software, you will be at a disadvantage. Your competitors will be operating faster and more efficiently than you.

Keep in mind too that hardware constantly improves while memory gets cheaper and chips get faster. At the same time reliability improves while prices fall. The computer industry considers a system more than three years old to be obsolete.

Chapter 2

THE MALLS

This chapter was originally going to be titled: "Is there a Nordstrom near you?"

Nordstrom, for those of you not familiar, is a large clothing and accessory department store known for its outstanding service. No, their prices are not the lowest. Customers who shop there think of Nordstrom as a store where the salespeople are helpful professionals.

Nordstrom's sales staff is, in my opinion, the best trained in the department store industry. Their attitudes, knowledge, personal attention, concern and consideration ensure the customer's satisfaction which results in repeat business and customer referrals. There is no better way to ensure success. Nordstrom has set the standard. If there is one near you and you haven't visited the store, I urge you to do so as soon as you can. You'll learn more about how to treat a customer in one visit than you will by spending days in sales seminars – mine included.

Perhaps Nordstrom has done shoppers a disservice. They've raised the expectations of the shopper to a standard few establishments can hope to duplicate. Just what are these expectations and how do they apply to those of us in the motorcycle and accessory business?

First, more people shop in malls, shopping centers and similar shopping complexes than anywhere else. Malls and shopping complexes have set the standard for physical appearance and cleanliness. They were, and are, designed by people who understood what makes consumers tick.

Little is left to chance. Starting with the demographics of their trading area, developers then consider the location, ease of access, availability of parking, and on and on.

They carefully select their tenants to create a mix aimed at attracting masses of people. They know that shopping can be transformed into a very pleasurable experience. The designers intend that once you visit the mall you'll make it an extended visit. They want you to stay around; visit more stores; have lunch or dinner; take in a movie and, most importantly, *spend money*.

We've Been "Malled"

Malls have changed the way Americans shop and have altered the consumer's perception of retailing. They have also raised the customer's expectations.

Clutter and dirt are no longer accepted. Sloppy displays and painted pegboard, once the standard for the motorcycle store, has become a decided handicap. Fluorescent lights that may be cost efficient, now must be replaced or at least augmented by high-tech accent lighting. Mirrors, once relegated to the bathroom, are an important, prominent showroom fixture. Why? Because today's shopper demands it.

Today's customers want SERVICE and, if the success of companies like Nordstrom is any indication, they are willing to pay for it. Today's customers want to be pampered and catered to. Today's customers want every convenience imaginable. Who are today's customers? We are.

Malls and shopping centers are competing for the dollars of today's customer, and they're fierce competitors. For us to get our piece of the pie, we must learn how to compete. We must also play their game; they've set the standard and established the expectations.

Mall stores open at 10:00 in the morning and stay open until 9:00 in the evening; they're open on Saturday and Sunday. The malls are not catering to the unemployed by closing at 5:00 pm. Too many of us appear to be unaware of not only why – but when people buy. The malls know we work all week and do most of our shopping on the weekend. They decorate for every holiday. Yes, the malls have created **GREAT EXPECTATIONS**.

To compete we must take a page out of their book. Go, visit a mall. When you do, concentrate not on what they're selling but on how they present their products. Look at their displays, the store layout, the lighting. Notice how the salespeople are dressed. Please look at their signs. Notice that few signs are about rules or regulations – **NO** checks, **NO** touching (no customers!) – except where mandated by law. Instead, they're eye catching and professionally done. By far the vast majority are aimed at inviting you to buy.

Is everything in your store priced? Every item sold in a mall is. Do you have special sales? The mall stores do. Did you decorate your store last St. Patrick's Day? Easter? Halloween? The mall stores did.

Serious Business

Why have the malls gone to such lengths? Competition for the consumer's dollar is serious business to them. In Eastern Europe there is a scarcity of almost all consumer goods. If, for example you lived in Poland and wanted to buy meat for dinner, you'd patiently stand in line. When it was your turn you'd be very nice to the butcher even if he smelled like a men's locker room, and was surly.

Where there is a shortage of goods, there is little competition among retailers for customers, and little motive to improve the quality of goods.

Like it or not, you're competing with the malls every day. Know and understand your competition. Be aware there are three things malls consider to be of prime importance.

1) Nothing happens by accident at the mall. Everything is done for a specific reason and purpose: to generate sales.

2) Mall owners want to make the shopper's visit an experience – and a pleasant and memorable one at that. Today it's all about the "customer experience." Mall owners understand what motivates their shoppers.

3) Malls know their weaknesses but they also know how to market their product.

The rules of the game say you must meet the customer's expectations. The rules say price is NOT the prime consideration: service and ambiance are. Learn to play by the rules. Meet the customer's expectations and be grateful you don't have to compete with Nordstrom.

Chapter 3

THE YELLOW PAGES

The Best Place To Advertise – Not!

Few people dislike the phone company more than I. My reason is not a rational one: they have a monopoly. I feel helpless, and, in most cases have no recourse when we disagree.

Most of the phone companies give me the impression that they are doing me a favor but can turn on me at any given time by doing such things as making the phone bill almost impossible to decipher and understand. Then they change their rates almost monthly and make it almost impossible for me to contact anyone with a pulse when I attempt to call them.

That being said, we still need the printed Yellow Pages. However, I now recommend that we place smaller ads and do so in more such books, not only in our immediate market but also perhaps in adjacent markets.

In the first edition of this book, written in the 1980s, I suggested that we use large Yellow Pages ads filled with information. That was before the Internet. Now I suggest the smallest possible ad with your address, phone number, hours and in big type: Web address.

My reasoning relates to recent studies that indicate people use the Yellow Pages to find phone numbers and not much else. Considering how much it costs each month to have an eye-catching ad I believe those dollars could be better spent on your Web site.

Instead of duplicating what's on your Web site in your Yellow Pages ad, use the Yellow Pages to drive consumers to your Web site. Keep your Yellow Pages ad simple, and instead put the detailed information in your Web site.

The advantages of your Web site over Yellow Pages are clear. You can update your Web site daily if you want, whereas you can't update the printed Yellow Pages ad except once a year. Web sites can be expanded almost infinitely by adding more pages. They will hold far more information than a Yellow Pages ad.

ONLINE YELLOW PAGES

Like most businesses today, the Yellow Pages also have ***online*** components. These are searchable sites that go by names such as SuperPages.com, BigYellow.com, SmartPages.com, Yahoo!Yellow Pages, Yellow.com, and similar URLs.

Many of the online Yellow Pages offer free business listings. You should take advantage of these free listings. They are one small way to create a strong Web presence for your business

Take an hour or two to visit as many of the online Yellow Pages as you can find through a search in Google. Check to see if your business is already listed. If not, enter your business information into the free listing section wherever you can.

Online Yellow Pages will also offer to sell you various kinds of enhanced listings and online ads, including pay-per-click ads (where you pay only if someone clicks through to your Web site). However, none of the online Yellow Pages can offer you the reach of the two giants in pay-per-click advertising: Google and Overture. You'd be wise to save your money for the big guys.

Chapter 4

FOLLOW-UP

Some very successful powersports dealers in large urban areas have found the cost of advertising in their market to be prohibitive.

Radio ads, they've told me, are too broad and not cost effective. TV is too expensive, and newspapers seem to be effective only for used units and deep discount sales. Web advertising can also be very expensive, costing thousands of dollars a month to maintain top position in search engines and buy online ads.

Despite this these same dealers have shown dramatic growth in an otherwise flat market. What are they doing differently? How can they attract new customers without getting out in the public eye? Their answer: intensive follow-up.

Here I've combined several different methods dealers have shared with me to produce a comprehensive, follow-up plan. Here's how it works.

Same Day

Step 1. Introduce the parts manager

Immediately after the unit is sold the salesperson introduces the customer to the parts manager. The parts manager then takes one of his business cards and writes on the back of it: To (the customer's name) you are entitled to a 10% discount on any parts or accessories you purchase. Valid until (date, 90 days from date of sale).

Handing this card to the customer the parts manager says: “This is my way of saying thank you for buying from us. This card gives you a 10 percent discount on any accessory or part you buy within the next 90 days. All you have to do is show me the card when you come in. Please don’t show it to anyone else at the counter. I can’t make this offer to everyone.”

Step 2. Introduce the service manager

The salesperson introduces the customer to the service manager. The service manager thanks the customer for buying the unit and pledges high quality and prompt service. He then gives the customer some small service-related gift.

It may be something as simple as a quart of oil. In that case, the service manager explains that this is the type of oil used in the engine of his motorcycle and says, “When an engine is new it may burn some oil. Take this with you and check your oil regularly. If it’s low, add some of this.”

The service manager then tells the customer that the unit was not made by God but by man, suggesting that there will be a need, covered under the warranty, for an inspection after just a short period of time...to tighten things up.

DAY TWO OR THREE

Step 3. Send the follow-up letter

Several days after the unit is delivered, the dealer sends the customer a hand-signed thank-you note and a gift certificate for $100 negotiable when the customer brings in a new buyer.

Two Weeks

Step 4. Make the first follow-up call

Two weeks later, the salesperson telephones the customer to ask about the bike and how he's is enjoying it. He also asks, almost as a "by-the-way," if the customer has shown his new possession to a friend, business associate or relative who may be a potential customer. The salesperson then offers to send this other person some literature. He asks permission to use the customer's name as a reference.

One Month

Step 5. The second follow-up call

A month after the customer takes delivery of his unit the parts manager telephones. He tells the customer of sales items and reminds him that the 10 percent discount is in addition to the sale price of the special.

Six Weeks

Step 6. The service department call

Two weeks after the parts manager calls the customer, the service manager telephones to ask about any mechanical problems that may have developed since he took delivery of his bike. Did he have to add the oil? Is there anything he has questions about? The service manager attempts to have the customer come in, at his convenience, so the vehicle can be inspected.

Step 7. The birthday card

Part of the paperwork includes the need to know the customer's birthday. Mark your calendar or enter that information into your computer database. The week before your customer's birthday, send him a card; no sales pitch, just a "Happy Birthday" card.

What do these seven steps do? They not only impress upon the customer that yours is a top-notch professional organization, but also guide him to the obvious conclusion that *you care*. He receives a letter and three phone calls from your dealership. When he returns to your store there are at least three people he can talk to. A customer who knows only the salesperson has a tendency to want to talk to that person even if the problem is not sales related. If the customer is introduced to the parts manager and the service manager, the salesperson's time will not be usurped as a go-between.

Happy Patrons Yak It Up

Two thirds of new, high-dollar "toys" are sold because of the recommendation of a satisfied customer. This, I believe, is the best possible reason for starting a comprehensive follow-up program.

Just as there are motorcycle retailers, there are follow-up companies who work under contract for dealers. They send boxes of cookies, flowers or candy along with a thank-you note and some other printed promotional material to your new customer. This follow-up, in my opinion, is cost effective and productive. The intense follow-up I've outlined here is, I believe, more effective because it's very personal.

One dealer said that in his thank-you letter he informs the buyer that his dealership produces a newsletter, and asks if he would like to be put on the mailing list. The dealer told me he never received a "no" answer to this question.

In a later chapter I talk about using email to send follow up communications. With answering machines and voice mail in common use today, it can be hard to reach customers by phone. An email is just as effective if not more. Be sure that you request the customer's email address at the time the sale is made, and enter it into your computer database.

Flop At Follow-Up

For reasons I'll never understand, few companies selling expensive "toys" consider follow-up to be as important as media advertising. A new customer, one who's still enthusiastic about his new toy, is like any recent convert. They want to tell others of their discovery.

You can take advantage of this honeymoon phase of your relationship by staying in touch. It's cheaper than radio ads, more focused than TV ads, and lasts longer than the newspapers.

In order to use this system, it will be necessary to produce a follow-up tool. Here you have a number of options, depending on your staff's technological sophistication. The tool can be on paper; in an electronic spreadsheet such as Excel; or fully automated using a contact management system or a customer relationship management (CRM) program.

For dealerships not used to using sophisticated technology tools, I suggest a simple paper system such as the one accompanying this section. The name, phone number, date of sale and description of unit purchased is written in columns across the top of the page, along with a list of the departments: sales, parts, service. As each department head has communications with the customer, the date is entered beneath the heading across from the customer's name. This is done to prevent the embarrassment of calling a customer only to have him remind you he was just in the store and saw you yesterday.

Who will opt to follow these seven steps? I suspect fewer than five percent of the readers of this book. Why? It's a lot of work. But then it's a lot of work to stay profitable all year 'round and through flat markets and increased competition. Survivors of "recessionary" cycles and high growth businesses are, historically, those retailers who differentiate themselves – pull away from the pack and make that extra effort in service to the customer.

Please note: the method described in this Chapter is not for the large dealer selling 100 or more units per month, because it requires

considerable hands-on attention. This method is best suited for smaller shops. Larger dealers should adopt similar follow-up programs, but rely on technology (follow-up emails, automated letters, and mailers) to automate portions of the process.

If you are one who puts the program into practice, please let me know how it works for you, and what refinements you would suggest to make it better.

FOLLOW UP FORM

FILL OUT UPON COMPLETION OF SALE

	CUSTOMER'S NAME	PHONE #	MAKE/MODEL YEAR	DATE	NEW?	SOLD BY	LETTER	SALES	PARTS	SERVICE	B/DAY	COMMENTS
1												
2												
3												
4												
5												
6												
7												
8												
9												
10												
11												
12												
13												
14												
15												
16												
17												
18												
19												
20												
21												
22												
23												
24												
25												

MIND YOUR OWN BUSINESS

Chapter 5

THE GREETING

"You never get a second chance to make a first impression." I don't know who first made that statement, but I believe it's true. It's also true that the pecking order is established within the first few moments of two people meeting each other.

Within the first minute or so, one of you will assume the position of being "in charge" – where you want to be – making that initial greeting of a customer the most important time in your relationship. These crucial few minutes set the tone for the relationship that follows.

What's the most common greeting in today's powersports store? "May I help you?" It's not only the most common; it's also one of the worst opening questions you can use. Why? Because the customer can, and often does, answer, "No thanks, just looking." When that happens, the salesperson loses, and the customer is in charge. The "NO" problem is so important I've covered it in a later chapter entitled, "OVERCOMING NO", so there's no need to discuss it further now.

If you agree that the initial meeting is important and you don't want a "NO" answer to questions, plan carefully and set the stage. Let's do that step by step.

Step 1. Your appearance

You must be appropriately dressed and wearing a name badge. Now the customer can tell who's who. Appropriate dress goes one step further in establishing a non-threatening, professional image.

Step 2. Wait one minute

Allow the customer a minute or two to look around and feel at ease. You'll create added tension if you rush up to someone before he has his bearings.

Step 3. Move in

Go to the customer, extend your hand and introduce yourself. If he doesn't respond instantly, don't force the issue. Some people have trouble shaking hands with a stranger. When you shake the customer's hand you'll probably notice that his hand is sweaty. That's a natural condition when someone is even slightly tense and out of their familiar surroundings. Unless you're comfortable, he won't be. Make your initial meeting personal, non-threatening, open and friendly.

Step 4. Learn his name

Learn the customer's first name and use it as soon as you can. Find a way to say his name at least three times during the first five minutes of conversation. Starting conversations with the other person's first name assures they'll listen.

Step 5. Ask questions

Never start by making statements about products. Your questions should allow the customer to talk and give you specific information. Find out about the customer; who he is and what experience he has, where he works, who he knows that you might know.

That's it! There are just five simple steps. If carefully followed, several things will become apparent to you.

1) You'll feel more comfortable because you'll know who's in charge ... <u>you</u>.

2) It will be easy and natural for you to smile during this first encounter since you'll be at ease.

3) You will establish a human bond by using the customer's name – particularly if he feels comfortable enough to use yours.

BE PREPARED

Before you greet your first customer using this five-step method, plan your questions. Decide in advance exactly what you'd like to know and when you want to know it. You'll want to know what the customer's interests are and if he is ready to take action. You'll also want to know if he can qualify for a large purchase and how much he knows about your products. Make a list of things it is important to find out and ask.

Continue to ask questions until you've learned what you need to know to make a definitive statement or guide the customer to a particular product. Besides getting the information you need, it encourages the customer to talk and perhaps reveal more than he intended. At the same time, it gives the customer the impression that you're professional.

Introverts account for about half our population. This group will become defensive and back off if they feel you're too aggressive. Extroverts can handle an aggressive approach, but you'll be taking an unnecessary risk if you're too familiar.

Physical action relieves tension. If you can get the customer to walk, even a short distance, the tension he feels will reduce dramatically. Handing him a piece of literature will also reduce tension and allows both of you to focus on something less personal than each other.

Some years ago the theory of the Zone of Personal Safety was the subject of a dissertation by a researcher in Pennsylvania. I confess that I don't remember the woman's name. However, the article was reported in *Psychology Today*, a respected monthly magazine. It was determined that people react involuntarily when meeting others in unfamiliar surroundings. Depending on the circumstances, everything is OK, according to the study, until the distance between the two parties becomes less than one arm's length, or about three feet. Once this zone has been broached, the person not in his own familiar surroundings or space, has a series of involuntary reactions. His pupils dilate; his heart rate increases. His temperature rises, as does his blood pressure. These involuntary reactions are similar to the animal response to the unfamiliar; fight or flight.

If we realize and accept these conditions as facts, we can see that the first few minutes are the most stressful for the customer. The need to reduce this stress should be obvious. Using the techniques I've outlined in this chapter, will help to establish a non-confrontational communications link between you and the buyer.

Chapter 6

SELECTING A WAREHOUSE DISTRIBUTOR

Dozens of warehouse distributors are competing for your business. Each has something special to offer. Selecting the "right" one for you will mean more profit dollars. It's more than just a simple case of who's got the lowest price. There is a formula that may help make the right choice.

At the IMAE (International Motorcycle Aftermarket Expo) show, several distributor salespeople were bemoaning the demand by dealers for the best price all the time. "Doesn't service count anymore?" they asked.

Prices are always a major consideration – particularly when they've been constantly increasing. Price wars, liquidation sales, and other promotions that use price as the drawing card are all too common in today's powersports market.

Dealers know that every accessory they sell is, from time to time, available for less money from someone else. Why? Distributor overstock, special manufacturer promotions, mistakes in purchases, discontinued product and the desire to extend distribution – to name just a few.

Prices should not be the sole criteria when dealers make purchasing decisions; our business is not that simple. The understanding of priorities and long-term goals between the parts buyer and the seller can create an environment for a mutually profitable relationship where price is only one of many factors.

Is there a right way to establish mutually beneficial working guidelines between the distributor's rep and the parts buyers? I believe there is. The buyer/seller relationship is based on agreements – some spoken, some implied – trust, and the willingness of two people to work together. It's up to the dealer and the distributor's rep to establish the ground rules.

This relationship, however, cannot be built on demanding the best price all the time, nor on the salesperson kicking back some of his hard-earned commission. It's built on trust, understanding, consideration and commitment.

Why would a dealer opt to use one particular supplier over the others as his major source of accessories or parts? Consider the following reasons.

Service Is King

Dealers are entitled to work with caring, informed, trained professionals. There's no reason to work with a WD rep just because he's "a good ol' boy." The dealers who have told me they like to spread their business around, are not being objective. Their reasoning sounds like a rationale for being unwilling to make a commitment. Worse, it's often a ploy to use one rep against another. If a dealer has five or six suppliers contacting him regularly, he should do business only with those who are truly willing to advise and help.

The distributor's representative who gets most of your business should have extensive product knowledge; be able to help you with displays, warranty claims, and be available to help with an open house or other special event. In short, he should act as an unpaid marketing assistant. If he is not willing to help in these areas, I recommend that you buy from someone who will.

A warehouse distributor's rep talks to hundreds of dealers, giving him the benefit of knowing what works and what doesn't. He should share this information with you. Of course you can't expect the rep to betray a confidence or divulge secret information about a competitor. But, he can be expected to show his customer the best way to display products; to aid in establishing realistic, competitive prices; to set up inventory levels; and to help you with in-store promotions and training. He should also be able to help you understand what Web resources are available from the WD or manufacturers in the form of online images, product descriptions and other information.

Published prices, unfortunately, show only your cost in dollars. Several factors will decrease the real effect on those prices. While it's impossible to quantify specific costs, consider the following formula:

S=P-[P*.05] W=P-[P*.02] D=P-[P*.03] H=P-[P*.02]=RC

Don't panic. That formula isn't as complicated at is looks, and after a brief explanation, I'll walk you through it step by step.

P = published price of product, S = service
Your true cost is reduced 5 percent (S=P-[P*.05] the first part of the formula) if you can count on getting first-rate service (S) from the warehouse distributor.

W = warranty and exchange
Subtract an additional 2 percent (W=P-[p*.02]) if the distributor offers a hassle-free warranty and exchange policy.

D = delivery and freight
The price decreases by 3 percent more (D=P-[P*.03]) if the distributor has a reasonable freight policy and can deliver promptly.

H = in-store help
Is the rep available to work during an open house? If so, product-cost declines another 2 percent (H=P-[P*.02]).

The real cost - (RC=real cost), is now much lower than the published price (P) if the distributor's rep can assure you he can offer all these services.

Let's use a real-life example of how my formula works. Let's say that the lowest published price (**P**) of a helmet is $100.00. First rate service (**S**) from your distributor will save you the equivalent of 5 percent, which is $5.00. If your distributor stands behind the product and helps with warranty claims and has a liberal exchange policy, you'll save another 2 percent, or an additional $2.00. If the distributor pays the freight and you get the helmet within two or three days (**D**), you will have saved another 2 percent, which is an additional $2.00. Finally, in-store help offered by the warehouse distributor's representative means you'll save 2 percent more. That's another $2.00 saving. Add those saving together and the real cost (**RC**) or the tire will not be $100.00 but $89.00.

What does all this mean? It means that you must take care when selecting your major suppliers. The better ones don't just sell products. A good working relationship between a distributor's rep and you can bring the published cost down by more than 10 percent, but only if you're a professional working with a professional.

Chapter 7

BUYING

If you bought 200 helmets last year and intend to buy 400 this year, you may be over-buying. If you bought 200 tires last year and have just bought 400 this year on spring dating, you may not be over-buying. Confused? Be patient, I'll explain.

Buying requires as much skill as selling; sometimes more. There are several categories of buying; they include special order purchases, stock replacement and stocking orders. Let's not worry about the first two because there's little risk of over-buying in these categories. The third condition, the stocking order, is where the skill and risk comes in.

The categories that control stocking orders are, or should be: **HISTORICALLY VALID, PROMOTIONALLY VALID,** and **FUTURIZING**. We will need to dissect these three to know which method you're using and discuss why you may want to change from one to another. You could be buying for the right reasons. Or, you could be doing it for all the wrong ones.

HISTORICALLY VALID BUYING

Let's take a hypothetical case. For each of the past three years you have bought and sold about 200 helmets annually. Your inventory this winter is about 50 helmets. It would be valid, based on history, to buy 100 helmets if the price and terms are favorable because you're likely to sell 100 during the next six months. If you have the credit to buy on spring dating, you'll be able to sell the helmets, make a profit and pay the distributor. You'll do all this with a minimum of risk – assuming, of course, that you will do the same amount of advertising and promotion as you did the previous years. Although I used helmets for this example, the same guidelines apply to batteries, spark plugs, tires, apparel or any family of accessories.

There are conditions over which you have no control that you must consider when you buy based on history. Conditions such as the competitive situation in your area. Are your competitors more or less aggressive than they were? Do you have more or less competition this year? Does a competitive dealer have an overstock you suspect he's ready to dump? What about the state of the general economy in your area? Is unemployment high? Do you anticipate things getting better?

If you feel confident there is no real outside threat, and the economy appears stable, you can buy with confidence. Historically valid buying is a conservative approach where there is little risk.

Dealerships run by managers with absentee owners and small dealers in competitive markets most often buy based on history. A store located in a rural area where there is a limited customer base and a potential for saturating their market should buy based on history.

You won't get rich quick using this method, but you'll be able to sleep nights. Your growth, if that's your aim, will be slow but controlled.

PROMOTIONALLY VALID BUYING

This method of buying requires more risk, but offers a greater potential reward. Using the same example as above, you might consider buying 400 helmets; double what you bought all last year. You'll probably get a better "deal" from the distributor in the form of more flexible terms and price concessions because of the volume. You're not over-buying if you're planning a promotion such as an open house, special sale or some other carefully planned activity designed to sell more helmets.

The open house or well-promoted sale will increase floor traffic and offer you the opportunity to sell not only the helmets, but close-outs, discontinued items, and special purchase accessories that have large profit margins. It's also a great way to create off-season cash flow.

If you have a good relationship with your WD rep (discussed in the previous chapter) you'll get his help with your event. Often, at the warehouse distributor's request, the manufacturer will send in a factory rep to participate in the event, if one is available. If one does show up at your store you'll be perceived by the consumer as having more "horsepower" than your competitors and as being an expert in helmets, for example. Once the promotion has ended, you'll find that helmets continue to sell well and may change your sales history for all your helmet lines.

When promotions become a regular part of your business, you'll notice a change in the attitude of your employees and customers. Everyone gets excited and "pumped" when they get involved in something special and different. It breaks the daily routine of a job and allows the creative juices to flow. It also helps the team spirit. Yes, the risk is higher. The excitement is also higher and the rewards are greater.

FUTURIZING

This third buying method is also the most dangerous and, unfortunately, the one relied upon by too many retailers. The synonym for "futurizing" is wishful thinking. Engage in this practice at your peril. If your WD sales rep is a futurizer and good talker, he may get you to over-buy because it seems like a good idea at the time. The logic he uses to convince you to buy the 400 helmets may sound good at the time, but may rest more on a "gut" feeling than pragmatic, well thought-out business reasons.

The rep who tells you his line of helmets is the "hot setup" and "there's going to be a shortage," should make you suspicious. Question the motives of anyone offering you a "once in a lifetime deal if you buy now and buy big." His motive may be a spiff from the manufacturer or based on a promotional sale by the warehouse. If the deal looks too good to be true, it probably is. Unless you have a plan to dispose of the product at a reasonable profit, pass.

Keep in mind, the WD and his rep have no risks other than the possibility you won't pay your bill. Unless he offers a guaranteed buy-back – something warehouse distributors seldom do – the risks are yours. Hunches, feeling and gut reactions are forms of gambling where the outcome is controlled by chance. A calculated risk is a reasonable and proper business decision where that risk can be weighed against the anticipated reward, and the outcome is influenced by your planned activity.

Whenever you contemplate making a large buy, concern yourself with the quantity and quality of the after-sale support you can count on from your supplier. If you do step up and buy, will the WD's rep work with you? Is there advertising support for the product on a national level? Has the rep sold this program to anyone else? If he did, call them and find out if there was an acceptable return on investment.

If you have a tendency to futurize, try to change to a more conservative approach as outlined in first two options. The best way to avoid futurizing is to wait. Don't make the buying decision on the spot. Insist on 72 hours before you commit to the program. Anyone who refuses to allow you this time has something to hide. You're not in the business of transplanting human organs where time is of the essence. Nothing in the retail powersports business is so pressing that it can't wait for 72 hours. Take that time and play devil's advocate. Write down all the reasons you can think of why it won't work, then all the reasons that it will. After that, write down what you'll have to do to make it work.

Translate what you've written into dollars; the dollars you have to spend to buy the helmets and the dollars of profit you can expect to make. Add the dollars you'll have to spend on the promotion: (Expected Profit less the added costs of advertising and promotion to assure those profits.) If the numbers don't work to produce an acceptable profit, don't do it. Even if the numbers do work, show what you've written to someone you respect. Do they agree with you? If you both feel it's worth the risk, it's your move.

Chapter 8

STEPS TO A SALE: "THE MAST"

Every book I've ever read on selling talks about the steps to a sale. Too few dealers in the powersports industry know those steps. Most I've met are "natural salesmen" who rely on their glib tongue and an instinctive knowledge of human reactions as their basic selling tools.

Few believe selling is a skill; most think of it as an art. How much does skill count? I'm told that 25 percent of all the salespeople in this country earn 75 percent of all the commissions. That means three fourths of the salespeople are left with only one fourth of the available commissions. Conclusion: Either you're good (which means skilled) or you're no good (which means unskilled). There is no middle ground. There are no mediocre salespeople; only good ones and bad ones.

If you're good, you're a professional; if you're not, you're an amateur. Professionals get paid; amateurs don't. It's tough to claim you're a professional if you are unaware of the basics steps to a sale.

Most of us have been just plain lucky at having developed an intuitive sense when selling. We've been getting along on our "natural" ability. Learn these steps and you'll improve your bottom line.

Interest, Attention, Action, Desire, Close – these were the five steps to a sale taught to sales people since the '60s. That method applied to commodities and necessities.

Things have changed. Today we know that powersports dealers are selling "wants" not needs. This has given rise to an opportunity to develop a new, easy-to-apply sales system. I call it the MAST method.

M stands for Meeting; the introduction stage.

A means the Ask stage; that portion of the presentation in which you ask questions to discover the customer's value system, lifestyle and history.

S represents the Show portion. Here's where "Show Time" comes in. This is the most important portion of the presentation. It involves the customer physically. The better the showman, the better the show. The better the show, the better the chances of a positive outcome. We'll discuss the Show step in more detail shortly.

T is for the Tell step. Remember back to your youth in grade school. The highlight of the day was the "show and tell" time.

When you become familiar with MAST selling you'll discover it's natural, easy, can be learned in a very short time, and put into practice almost immediately. If each section is isolated and practiced, the result will be more sales, more referrals and more enjoyment. There is, however, a need for discipline in order to stay in control of the process.

OK, now let's dissect the process.

Meeting Stage

The meeting or greeting of a new customer sets the tone for the rest of the presentation. It also sets the rules for the relationship between the customer and the salesperson. It allows the salesperson to make a positive first impression.

Remember that old saying: "You never have a second chance to make a first impression." The meeting stage should be informal. It should acknowledge the customer's presence and indicate you are pleased to have him in your store. A simple "Hi, come on in and look around, I'll be with you in a minute," is often all you need to do. Selling or attempting to sell product is inappropriate at this stage.

Now it gets a bit more critical. You MUST wear your name tag. You must become a person in the eyes of the customer. That person must have an identity. It is not the customer's responsibility to remember your name. The nametags will be a constant reminder. Besides, it lets the customer know who works there. Research has shown that it is five times more difficult for someone to turn you down if they know you by name.

ASK STAGE

As soon as the Meeting/Greeting stage has been achieved, the Ask portion is the next step. Here's where you become the expert. What do you ask? Questions that are designed to gain information.

Never, never ask a question that can be answered with a simple "no." Why? It ends conversation and takes control away from the salesperson. Instead, ask questions to discover things about the customer.

The Ask stage should be the portion of the presentation where the customer does most of the talking, and you do most of the listening. If we reduced it to ratios, I'd suggest you talk one-third of the time and allow the customer to talk two-thirds.

What should you want to know? Where the customer lives and works. You should find out if the customer has been in your store before; if they own a motorcycle or watercraft now, or have owned one in the past. What did they own, when did they own it, how did they like it?

These questions are non-threatening and allow the customers to reveal something about themselves. Spend as much time on this portion as the customer seems to feels appropriate.

Knowing, for example, that a person hates the color green could save you from a difficult situation if you began to extol the virtues of a particular unit, which happened to be green. Perhaps color selection is not important to you. However, it may be very important to someone else. Knowing that different people like different things for different reasons and knowing what those things are will give you a tremendous advantage. The only way to know is to ask.

Once you have asked the question, wait. Don't continue to talk. Give the customer the chance to think and then respond. Some people find it difficult to communicate with strangers and need to be encouraged. The best way to encourage a response is to ask the question again, perhaps rephrasing it.

Show Stage

Now for the biggie – the Show time. This is the action portion of the presentation. This is the portion that gets the customer physically involved with the product. This is show business. The show portion of the process makes the presentation both fun and interesting,

Now that we've passed through the Ask step, it is important to minimize asking questions. Now you have to tell or inform the customer. Just as in your grade school days, show and tell are combined.

For example, instead of asking the customer if he would like to sit on the motorcycle or try on the jacket, tell them. "Here, try this on," has a better chance of success than asking: "Would you like to try this on?" "Sit on the motorcycle and see for yourself how comfortable the saddle is," will have a better outcome than: "Would you like to sit on it to see how comfortable it is?"

The Show stage involves features and benefits. Features are physically properties of a product. They can't stand alone. They must be tied into a benefit to the customer. Here's where we can show our expertise and sensitivity. Here's also where we have a tendency to talk too much.

"Actions speak louder than words," so act. Involve the customer in the action. A show that involves action and customer participation is a show that will never close for lack of a paying audience. The Meeting when followed by the Asking step sets the stage for the Show. Now you know what your audience's (customer's) likes and dislikes. You know his preferences and values. Knowing your audience is the secret to a successful presentation.

The Show stage represents the emotional component. Emotions – not intellect – press the customer buying trigger.

We're in the business of selling dreams, escapism, and fantasy. These things are not intellectual, they're **emotional**.

The Show should involve mostly non-verbal senses: touch, sound and visual images. The more senses involved, the more emotion becomes the trigger. Dreams and fantasies are not intellectual, neither is the decision to buy a motorcycle, watercraft, snowmobile, accessories or any emotionally fulfilling leisure product.

The Show involves such values as pride of ownership. It also has a great deal to do with the feeling of self-worth. A haphazard Show is no show at all. One that's practiced and considered allows the showman to stay in charge of the presentation.

Tell Stage

The last step is the Tell portion. Tell involves that most horrible phrase "the close." Any questions asked at this stage should be asked for agreement only. If you asked the appropriate questions early on, the questions you ask at this stage should be presented with the goal of moving toward a successful conclusion ... the sale. When you develop self-confidence, you'll discover that you won't find it necessary to ask many questions at this juncture. "Come in the office, and we'll take a look at the numbers," a strong but confident tell statement. "Press hard, you have to go through five carbon copies," is a strong tell statement that's also a challenge.

If the customer is not in the frame of mind to accept your tell statements, he will soon let you know. Perhaps, during the question or Show portion of the presentation the customer was distracted. Perhaps you were distracted or interrupted. That may have left some unanswered questions in the customer's mind. The Tell stage is where those uncertainties can surface. Staying in control is very important.

When the customer indicates he does not have sufficient information, go back to the Ask step. Make sure all the questions have been addressed; that the customer has no more substantive issues to resolve. Then, move on.

There is another benefit of the Tell phase. Tell means you have stopped selling. Too many of us feel impelled to continue to sell after the sale is over. Put another way, we sometimes make our point and then continue to talk, thereby blunting it. I've seen sales evaporate in the confusion created by an overload of information.

The tendency to sell, sell, sell, and never stop is responsible for the customer feeling pressured by the salesperson. Buyer's remorse can be avoided if the customer feels he has made his decision with guidance not pressure.

Chapter 9

TRICKS

Selling is a skill and a profession. To be good at it you must know what stimulates a consumer and prompts his first visit to your store.

Auto dealers know what motivates most of their customers. They know, for example, that the average car buyer harbors a strong distrust of auto salespeople. (From my personal experience, I'd say with good reason.) They also know that the customer is more likely to buy if he believes the dealer is in a bind and needs to get rid of inventory. In other words, they'll buy if they think they can beat the dealer at his own game. To get a customer into this frame of mind, the advertising must create an imminent response condition.

An automobile or powersports dealer who advertises that his "Entire inventory must be sold regardless of the loss," is probably lying, but he will generate more floor traffic than his neighbor who advertises service, quality or convenience.

Few powersports dealers play this traffic-building game. However, a store filled with inventory needs floor traffic, and the more, the better. YOU must supply the motive for people to want to visit you. YOU must convince the customer to rush to your store NOW. Let's examine some of the different sales tactics used to motivate. The following examples require immediate response. They are the "DO-IT-NOW" programs other industries have been using for years.

The Distress Sale

A sale that lasts a specific, short period of time with discounts which appear excessive. Often, prices are inflated and then heavily discounted. The customer who buys "deals" only, will feel he can take advantage of you and save money at the same time and responds to the distress sales. Some common catch phrases used are:

1. "Ten units must be sold today regardless of profit. What we don't get rid of during this sale will be wholesaled to another dealer."

2. "We overbought, and must reduce our inventory to pay our suppliers by Friday. We even accept unreasonable offers."

The Sales Contest

A sale that appears to benefit the store, not the customer. It gives the impression that you're more interested in sales than profits. A few catch phrases are:

1. "If we sell just three more the boss gets a trip to Hawaii."

2. "We're going to be number one in our district even if we have to lose money on the next 10 sales to do it."

Make Room Sale

A sale that leads the customer to believe that you're out of space and need room, not profit. Catch phrases:

1. "We bought another dealer's inventory and have no place to put it."

2. "We bought factory closeouts and need space."

3. "We lost the lease on our warehouse and must sell off the inventory."

THE GET EVEM SALE

A sale whose motivation appears to be revenge. It seems you are more interested in getting even than making money. Catch phrases include:

1. "Customers tell us that other dealers are underselling us. Not anymore. For the next 10 days we guarantee we won't be undersold even if we have to sell for cost or less."

2. "The factory said we are not selling enough units. OK, we'll sell the next 10 units at cost to protect our franchise. First-come, first-served."

The obvious motive in these examples is more sales of units. The customer who buys if he feels he can beat you at your own game responds to these techniques. This genre of customer insists on buying at the best possible price and if you lose money, that's OK with him.

This is a strong condemnation of the state of retail selling today; however, this method of building traffic by deception has become the norm. Today's big-ticket customer has been conditioned to expect it. As a result, today's buyers show little respect for salespeople. Automobile and powersports salespeople receive a level of respect just slightly higher than that given to an insurance or vacuum cleaner salesman.

Is this type of advertising dishonest? Yes it is. Is it common? Yes it is. Who uses these methods? Retailers in just about every industry.

An airline advertises: "Fly to Chicago for only $129!" Then in small print, they add; "Some restrictions apply. Seats limited." You call the airline and discover you must buy your ticket a month in advance, stay at least 14 days, and the low-priced seats are sold out until next April. "But, as long as you're on the line, we'll give you the best possible price consistent with your travel plans," they'll sweetly tell you. You'll end up paying $350 for the "$129" fare.

Department stores and mass merchandisers use these methods regularly with less-than-honest clearance, special-purchase, warehouse and remodeling sales. Large companies have been successfully sued by states because of illegal sales advertising practices. Even the big ones have been targets of consumer protection agencies in several eastern states.

Misleading and yes, even downright dishonest sales, are part of the American retail marketing scene.

The state of New York had to adopt laws prohibiting retailers from having "Going Out Of Business" sales unless they were truly going out of business. Why? Some stores advertised they were going out of business for more than 10 years.

Sellers Beware

Should you use one of these methods? That depends on how much floor traffic you want and your philosophy of selling. If you're active, involved, offer real service and not just lip service, it won't be necessary. You can probably get all the floor traffic you need using more honorable methods.

My personal opinion? Take care when operating in the "gray area." There's a line between sales hype and a swindle. The former may be an acceptable exaggeration; the latter a punishable crime. If you're not sure, check with the Better Business Bureau or your attorney.

"Bait and switch" advertising in which a low-priced product (usually not all it's cracked up to be) is offered for sale to lure customers, is used by airlines, auto dealers, computer stores and audio stores, among others. It is a gray area, but it appears these companies find it a useful tool to build sales. Take care not to cross the line.

Don't be afraid to sell sizzle to bring people into your store. Honesty is important, but don't feel you have to be so honest as to ignore showmanship. Showmanship and magic ... people love it.

Chapter 10

THE RIP-OFF

I hate getting ripped off, so do you, and so does everyone else. To make matters worse, we all know that at one time or another, we've been victims of the rip-off. We have been overcharged for products or services and when we discovered it ... we got mad! Our first thoughts were for revenge. That might not be noble, but it's the human condition. We know that motorcyclists don't often get mad. They do, however, get even.

If we all detest getting ripped off, why are some of us willing to rip-off our customers? In these times of Internet sales where competitors can be in another state, customers are not easy to come by. Ripping them off may bring in some much needed cash flow for a little while, but the long-term cost may be more than you've bargained for.

Are you the victim or the one doing the ripping? Some mail-order companies claim that at least part of their increased sales are due to consumers believing they've been ripped off by their local retailers. They've opted to try mail order as an alternative, feeling they may be safer. Does this perception have any validity? I've discovered it does. Worse, I've found that some people in our industry are teaching dealers how to rip-off customers.

A while back a dealer phoned me asking for help. He was losing money. Fewer customers were buying, or even visiting the store. One of the things I did when I visited this dealer was to phone several dozen of his customers who hadn't been seen in his store lately. The dealer told me they used to be "regulars."

At first, my attempt to get the former customers to talk to me was thwarted by their reluctance to tell me anything substantive. After just a few calls, I decided to change my approach. From then on, I identified myself as an outsider trying to find out why the person was avoiding the store.

"I got tired of being ripped off!" One ex-customer said. I asked him to tell me exactly how he was ripped off. It took some probing, but eventually the customer told me the dealer charged him $5 every time he wanted to buy something that was not in stock. "He called it a warehouse transfer fee," the ex-customer told me. "The first time I figured it was because I'd ordered something that took special handling. Then I found out he was charging everyone the $5 fee if he didn't have the parts on hand. That's a rip-off. It isn't my fault if the dealer doesn't carry enough inventory."

Several more customers told me similar stories. I asked the dealer to explain: "I attended a seminar given by Mr. Pundit (not his real name). He said I could make more profit if I charged the customers what he called a 'warehouse transfer fee,'" the dealer said. "He told us that most customers would accept the additional cost and we'd help our bottom line."

"Did you make more profit?" I asked.

"Oh yes...I did, he said. "When I got my year-end P&L it showed my parts and accessory margin of profit was up more than 10 percent from the previous year."

"OK, then what?" I asked, waiting for the punch line.

"Well. . .this year I showed a still higher percentage of profit but my total parts and accessory sales were down almost 40 percent and floor traffic has been down all year," he went on.

"Do you feel the increase in your profit margins and the decrease in your sales are related?" I asked, believing I knew what he would answer.

"I don't know. That's why I called you," he said.

Later that day we drafted a letter to all this dealer's customers. The letter told of a policy change and offered to make amends in the form of discounts for any previous customer who felt he had been abused by the "fee."

This dealer is a sincere person who has been in business a long time. He is dedicated and is, himself, an enthusiastic motorcyclist. He admits he put profits before morality and knows it's going to be a long haul back to profitability.

If you're engaging in this type of rip-off, please, please re-consider. Your customers are not stupid. They may not complain, but they may not return. They may even feel it's OK to steal from you because you're stealing from them.

As you'll read in chapter 13, "The P.O. Factor," if they like you they'll tell three other people. If they don't like you, they'll tell 11 others. When a customer feels he has been ripped off, I suspect that number 11 may double.

Beware of the Mr. Pundits in any industry who advise you to do what you know in your heart is immoral, dishonest or unfair. Put yourself in your customer's shoes before you make marketing decisions. If you wouldn't want it to happen to you, why do it to someone else?

Chapter 11

STICKER SHOCK

Sticker shock has caused more than one powersports manufacturer to react and roll back prices. Offshore manufacturers have reduced their profits to what some business economists consider unacceptably low levels. They've done it partly to reduce sticker shock – that look of disbelief on a customer's face the moment he sees the price of a product. It hasn't worked. The dollar has sunk too low. You can expect to see prices rise still higher in years to come.

The U.S. dollar, when compared with most European countries' and Japanese currency, is low. Economists are predicting that the U.S. dollar will probably remain unstable for years to come. As the common market in Europe becomes more of a factor, and the United States trade deficit continues, the pressure on the dollar will remain strong.

The weak U.S. dollar is arguably, the largest problem being faced by some off-shore powersports and accessory companies alike. However, it's a boon to many American manufacturers and exporters. During the last election we heard politicians place blame for this condition on our national debt and the other political party.

This chapter won't address world economics for one basic reason: I know almost nothing about the subject except what I read in the papers and see on the TV financial programs. However, I do know that every foreign motorcycle manufacturer and importer lives in fear of consumer sticker shock on imported items from apparel to zoom lenses.

At the root of their fear is the likelihood that the retail price of their products will rise to a level that will adversely affect sales. In other words, the products will become so expensive customers won't buy them; a legitimate concern.

If the problem is so great, why do so many dealers exacerbate it? They don't do it intentionally, but they do it. Let me give you an example and then show you how to reduce or even eliminate sticker shock.

Sticker Shock Strikes

Recently I was called in by a first-class motorcycle and watercraft dealer to help with a sales problem. Used bikes were selling well, but new ones were gathering dust in the showroom while accumulating floor-plan interest. Everything in the store was well done, from the lighting to the displays; the professionalism of the sales staff to the layout of the service department. I thought I'd have to delve deeply into the dealership to discover the problem. I was wrong.

While I was in the office with the owner, a man, who I'd guess to be about 40, came in. He walked over to a loaded tourer and let out a gasp. "Nineteen thousand dollars! That's three times what I paid for a bike just like this less than 10 years ago!" Before either of us could do anything he was out the door, in his car, and gone.

I went to the sales floor to see what caused his panic. There it was! I knew immediately why the dealer was having a problem selling new bikes. The hang-tags displayed on all his new bikes were causing instant, terminal, sticker shock.

Because this dealer was conscientious and thorough, the handlebar hang-tag was filled with information. The specifications, along with features and benefits, were printed on the tag. Also on the tag was a bunch of numbers with dollar signs in front of them. They included the cost of the added accessories, freight, setup, taxes and license tag. So what was the big problem? Written with a wide, black, felt tipped pen, in **HUGE** numbers was "$19,340.50 Total Price." It was written across the biggest portion of the hang-tag.

The customer, or rather the prospective customer who'd just left the store, had bypassed all the other information and focused on those large, frightening numbers.

Suppose the dealer opted to remove the hang-tags and show no prices on the bikes. Would that solve the problem? No! It might even make matters worse. People have become accustomed to seeing prices on everything from groceries at the supermarket to window stickers on cars. Unpriced, large-ticket items create suspicion in the minds of cautious buyers. Vehicle salespeople are perceived by the general public to be untrustworthy. However, the printed word is thought to be honest. To avoid the natural suspicion of a defensive customer, prominently display printed prices. Since the automobile and truck industry were forced to display prices shoppers have come to expect to see prices, not just hear them.

Without printed prices on the hang-tags, a salesman busy with a buyer may be interrupted by another customer asking about the price of a particular motorcycle. If the salesman gives him the price, the new customer will probably leave before anyone has a chance to discuss features, benefits, terms or anything else. If the salesman refuses to answer the question directly the customer will, in all likelihood, become annoyed or suspicious, and react by leaving. Priced hang-tags therefore, appear to create a "catch 22."

Avoiding The Syndrome

Half the dealers I've talked to about this subject have price tags on their inventory; half don't. Each has valid reasons for his choice.

A hang-tag is important and should be displayed on all new and used bikes available for sale in the showroom or outside on the lot. The information they relay to the customer is important. However, the way that information is presented will make all the difference in the world.

What information should be on the hang tag? The features and benefits of the unit; a statement that says "As little as;" information on the next step the customer should take.

FEATURES AND BENEFITS

The features and benefits of the unit should be described as fully as possible using typed or printed small letters and numbers. If necessary use the back of the hang-tag to list these.

AS LITTLE AS

Then, using a broad-tipped felt pen, scrawl across the entire lower portion of the tag the following: "As little as $150 per month." Using the term "as little as" avoids the necessity of listing the percentage of down payment and the number of monthly payments.

TAKE ACTION

"See Ed or Jim for details." Of course Ed and Jim (store salesmen) should be wearing nametags to identify themselves. The $150.00 example may not be actual numbers used. The monthly payment should be calculated based on a 20 to 25 percent down payment and the longest time-payment schedule available.

When there are five numbers in front of the decimal point, it's sure to trigger the sticker-shock syndrome. The trigger won't be pulled if the customer sees three little numbers before the dot, representing monthly payments.

When I discussed this with the dealer, he thought that was a sneaky, or at least a less-than-honest way of doing business. It's not; it's real-world selling. Monthly payments are a way of life, and reflect on the way most people live, work and buy.

Working people get paid by the week or month. They spend the same way. Stressing monthly payments has become the selling norm for major purchases. However, full disclosure is seldom offered before the customer has come to the decision to buy. If full disclosure were required prior to commitment the real estate market would collapse.

Suppose a real estate salesman was forced to be as informative as this motorcycle dealer. Here's what he would have to tell a prospective buyer of a house with a market price of $70,000. "Yes sir, this $70,000 house is only going to cost you $229,526. Sign here." Would you sign? Of course not. However, the $229,526 figure is what the house will cost you over the next 30 years based on $5,000 down, and an interest rate of 11 percent plus two points. The interest alone is over $160,000; more than twice the price of the house. Add taxes and insurance for 30 years and the number is even higher. If the customer had this information before making his purchase decision, chances are he'd never become a first-time home owner.

The total price should never be the dominant feature of a hang-tag. Stressing monthly payments minimizes sticker shock and diminishes the difference between you and your competition. Although your price may be as much as a $1,000 more than your competitors, that difference becomes about $20.00 per month when translated into time payment terms.

With properly prepared hang-tags, the new prospect will be able to evaluate the differences in bikes based on their features and benefits without becoming overly concerned with the "total drive out price." He may even discover there's only $40 or $50 per month difference between what he might have been willing to settle for and what he would really want to own. The information printed on the tag has another benefit too. As mentioned earlier, if you're busy with someone when the new prospect comes into the store, it will allow him to occupy and inform himself until you're available to help him.

Please note: the above applies to displaying merchandise for sale in a retail setting. Don't confuse this with financing disclosures given at the time the consumer decides to finance his purchase. In that case, make sure you are following the disclosures required by law and your lending facility.

Chapter 12

HOW TO VUE THE CUSTOMER

Before you jump to the conclusion that I can't spell (in truth, I use a word processor with a spell checker), the word **VUE** is an acronym I created.

VUE stands for **V**alidate, **U**pdate, **E**ducate. Learning to use this tool will improve the professional's "hit rate." The term hit rate (I made that one up too), refers to the number of sales per customer contact.

Before we get into **VUE**, let's define hit rate. If, for example, you visit with 10 potential customers and write orders for three, your hit rate is 30 percent. Few salespeople engaged in selling major ticket items, such as motorcycles or watercraft, ever experience a hit rate of over 30 percent. Counter people selling parts and accessories can, and often do, have hit rates of 75 percent or more.

VUE is best described by showing examples of how it's used. I'd like to share with you two such real life experiences where the **VUE** method was successfully used.

A customer was about to make a purchasing decision on a rather expensive touring bike. Everything seemed to be going well until the customer asked about the finish. When the salesman said the unit had a urethane finish over the color, the customer gasped. "That's dangerous stuff. I just read an article that told of a case where a man almost died because he had the bike with a urethane finish stored in his unvented garage. The story said the urethane finish created some sort of poison gas!"

The salesman thought the customer was joking. Fortunately, he didn't burst out laughing. Instead he **Validated** the customer's concerns by telling him that urethane, like most finishes, is hazardous and care has to be taken when it's applied in liquid form. He assured the customer that once dry there was no danger.

The salesman asked if perhaps the story was about someone applying urethane in an un-vented garage. The customer admitted he might have misread the article – perhaps it did talk about applying the finish.

The salesman then decided to **Update** the customer by discussing the different types of finish material, and the features and benefits of each. In this instance, updating and educating overlapped. The assurance given to the customer by the sales person was all it took to close the sale.

What do you think would have happened if the salesman had just laughed? Would he have made a sale? Of course not.

In another example, a customer said he decided not to buy a particular brand of motorcycle because he "heard that if you have a problem with that brand you can't get replacement parts." The dealer's first reaction was to respond with equal hostility. Although he didn't say it to the customer, he told himself he was dealing with an opinionated, close-minded jerk. Rather than confront the customer the salesperson found a way to agree with him. The salesman **Validated** the customer's opinion.

He told the customer of a case where a particular model, which had never sold well, and had been discontinued years before, did have such a problem. "A customer who owned one needed parts which were not available from the manufacturer," the salesman said. "We had to have the parts machined for him."

Then the **Update** process began. The salesman assured the customer that he wouldn't have that problem with this model. "It's been on the market for almost 10 years and we have a large stock of parts. What we don't have we can get from the factory in just a few days," he told the customer. He continued the **Update** process by showing the customer the store's inventory of parts, and pointed out how many of that particular model the dealership had sold over the past several years. The customer was satisfied with the explanation.

The next step was to **Educate** the customer, which put the salesman firmly in control. He showed the customer the computer order system the store used, and explained how quickly they could get replacement parts for out-of-service motorcycles. The **VUE** system worked. The customer's opinions were not challenged, but validated. He was then updated and educated. He bought.

VALIDATE

You cannot, and should not, invalidate a customer's feelings. If he expresses a feeling about something, even if that feeling is negative, don't argue. No one wins an argument. Instead, find a way to **Validate** that feeling. Nothing takes the wind out of the sails of an impending argument faster than having the parties agree with each other. Once it's evident that you and the customer are on the same side, you will have the opportunity to **Update** him.

UPDATE

This step takes a considerable amount of product knowledge. It also requires a keen sense of history. What was true yesterday may well be false today. You won't know when or where your customer discovered his "facts." Perhaps, when he first heard them, they were truly facts. Today, however, because of the march of technology, things have changed.

EDUCATE

This intangible can dynamically increase sales. **Education** allows customers to make decisions based on information you provide. You're the expert. If you have the information and present it in a non-threatening manner, the customer will feel less anxiety and hostility. Buying then becomes easier and more pleasant.

Customers seldom have up-to-date information. If they read it in a magazine it's at least three months old. When a friend tells them of a bad experience, the problem may have taken place years ago. Carefully update the customer with the latest information.

Before you use the **VUE** method on an unsuspecting prospect determine the information you want by asking the appropriate questions. What does the customer know, and where did he obtain his information. You'll need to ask these questions in a non-threatening, non-hostile way. No matter how silly the answers seem to be to you, take care that you don't laugh. Here's where real professionalism shows.

We know that customers are rarely experts in the powersports field. There is more invalid information floating around than valid knowledge. Anyone who's been in this business for more than two years knows that to be a fact.

Learn to **VUE**. It will become your major sales tool and increase your professionalism.

Chapter 13

THE P.O. FACTOR

It's the customer's money
that keeps our businesses solvent.
The customer is ***always*** *right.*

No Martha, we're not talking about Purchase Orders. Yes. We're talking about the piss-off factor – the alienation of a customer to a point where there's a confrontation and the customer vows he will never set foot in your store again.

Everyone in the retail business (you're really in the retail business, not in the powersports business) knows that the best source of new customers is an existing, satisfied customer. When a referred customer visits you, your chances for a sale are much higher than someone who just picked up the phone book or happened to stop by.

Research has shown a satisfied customer considers it an obligation to tell three other people; that is, they'll happily tell friends, acquaintances, business associates and just about anyone else that yours is the place to buy.

What few powersports retailers realize is that same customer, if dissatisfied, will likewise make it his social responsibility to advise, inform or warn eleven other people to stay away from your store. If we continue this numbers game, here's what we'll find. Take your customer base and, if all your customers like you, multiply by three. Goodwill can, if you believe this formula, increase your business 300 percent.

Now, let's look at the other side of the coin. If the **P.O.** factor has reared its ugly head and your customers now dislike you, multiply your base by negative 11. The result: you're out of business!

It's easy to see that neither of these extremes is common.

IN REAL LIFE

I've used outrageous examples to get your attention. Now we can look at the real world of retailing in the motorcycle, watercraft, snowmobile and accessory business. We'll examine the **P.O.** factor as part of the human condition.

Most people are reasonable. Most are considerate and honest. Most will behave as you expect them to. Most people do, however, become emotional, unreasonable and act irrationally from time to time. You and I are included in "most people." No one knows for sure what causes irrational behavior. Perhaps it's the pressure of Life in these trying times.

We know that we're in the business of supplying wants, not needs. This means we're dealing with emotions as much as, or more than, intellect. Dealing with the emotional side of people can turn solid ground into quick-sand. Say the wrong thing and an otherwise thoughtful person may suddenly get P.O.-ed.

How can you avoid triggering the P.O. factor? There are several rules you must accept. These are tough rules, and you may find it's difficult to follow them. But you must if growth and service are not just words to you.

Rule 1 The customer is always right. (More on this later.)

Rule 2 Argue, and you lose.

Rule 3 When a disagreement surfaces ask the customer what would make him happy... then DO IT!

Rule 4 You'll never make a profit from a dissatisfied customer.

Rule 5 You will probably lose money trying satisfying a dissatisfied customer.

Rule 6 Never insist on being right, even if you are!

Here are a few examples of how the P.O. factor – or avoiding it – changes your profit picture.

Avoiding P.O.

A powersports dealer in upper Michigan told me of a good customer who came to the store and bought a voltage regulator. Several days later the customer returned with the regulator and asked for his money back. His reason? He discovered the problem was not in the charging system. It was a loose connection to the battery.

The dealer tried to explain that he couldn't make a refund on electrical items. He pointed to the sign behind the counter to support his position. The customer stood his ground. The P.O. factor was about to be triggered. The dealer gave the customer back his money thereby avoiding the P.O. factor, and bigger losses down the road than his investment in the regulator, I assure you!

Three weeks later the customer returned. This time he apologized, related a story of how the problem must have been more than just the battery cable. It seems the bike died when the customer was riding 50 miles from home. It cost him a small fortune to have the biked towed back to town. He said he had learned his lesson and sheepishly asked if the dealer would find and take care of the problem. This story ended well.

Triggering P.O.

A customer left his new touring bike to be serviced. The dealer told him it would be ready on Friday. Friday afternoon the customer returned only to be told that some needed parts were back ordered by the supplier. The customer exploded (figuratively speaking) and demanded to know why he wasn't called before he made the trip. Then he accused the dealer of being inefficient, inconsiderate and lazy.

The dealer accused the customer of being hot headed and unrealistic. The result? A first class P.O. factor. The dealer lost the customer forever. The problem could have been avoided if; the dealer had called before the customer made the trip, or the dealer apologized for not calling and asked to be forgiven for this oversight.

AVOIDING P.O.

A week after the customer had his engine completely rebuilt he returned to the dealer with the bike on a trailer. He was furious. The bike got him home alright but he could never get it started again. He launched a diatribe against the dealer. The dealer took all the wind out of the customer's contention by agreeing that the experience must have been awful.

A service technician was called out immediately. Upon inspection it was found that the coil wire had slipped out. The repair was made in less than a minute, and the bike ran just fine. The dealer then apologized to the customer claiming that he (the dealer) should have spent more time checking over the unit. The now embarrassed customer listened intently and then admitted he was less than mechanically inclined and probably "flew off the handle." He thanked the dealer for the prompt service and attention.

The result? No P.O. factor and the dealer has a valued customer on his side.

Remember, it's the customer's money that keeps our businesses solvent and thriving. The customer can spend his dollars wherever he wants. We MUST cater to, and service the customer. If you look back at Rule #1, you'll see that "the customer is always right." If you don't think the customer is always right, go back and read all the rules again.

Chapter 14

TAKE IT IN TRADE

Everything has a value. No matter what the item, it can be sold to someone for some amount of money. As one wag once said: "For every seat there's an ass." So, don't be afraid to take it in trade. Take what in trade? Anything!

A Yamaha dealer I met once told me how he took four cows in trade on a new Yamaha. He then called the local newspaper. The story appeared on the front page. It was later picked up by the wire service and printed in newspapers as far away as France. This one event, according to the dealer, was responsible for his business becoming profitable after years of drifting.

There's a Harley-Davidson dealer in remote western Canada who was having trouble because of the economy in his market. One day a farmer dropped by the store and expressed an interest in buying a bike. However, he didn't have any money. After some discussion, the dealer discovered the farmer had several hundred acres of wheat under cultivation. He asked the farmer to bring in a sample.

Later that afternoon the farmer returned with a sample of the unripe grain. The dealer had it assayed at a local grain supplier, to determine how much it was worth and found a customer who was willing to buy it. He offered the farmer a price, and made the deal. The dealer's net profit was more than double what he would have made if he had sold the bike for the full price.

This dealer told me he now makes more money trading in, and selling, livestock and grain, than he ever did just selling motorcycles. Once he decided he wasn't in the motorcycle business but in the business of making a living things improved.

I've been told similar stories by dealers in New Mexico and Texas – at a time when those two areas had been suffering because of the decline in the oil industry. These dealers regularly take diamond rings, cars, real estate and firearms in trade. They've also told me that their net profit, when they deal this way, is better than selling the bike for full price. Do they know something we don't? I think so.

As Sherman Barnett, a Harley dealer in El Paso, Texas, explained it this way: "The customer is interested in owning a motorcycle. He wants to obey the buyer's eleventh commandment: 'Thou shall not pay full price.' Everyone wants a deal. When a customer is thinking about buying, he rarely considers trading in, or selling something he owns, but doesn't use or need any longer. That's why taking it in trade is a good idea."

Is that a valid observation? I think it is. Have you ever gone to a garage sale? If you have you'll notice that when someone no longer has a need, or want for something, they'll sell it for a small fraction of its actual worth. I've bought a set of $1,500 stereo speakers for less than $100 because the man having the garage sale had just gone through a divorce, had sold his house was moving into an apartment. The speakers were too big, and besides, he had to share the proceeds with his ex-wife.

I've been surprised to find that more often than not, the customer has a lower perceived value of an item he wants to be rid of than its real worth. I've also discovered that many dealers offer too much when taking in trades, particularly non-motorcycle trades. The customer wants to spend less money. If you encourage him to trade something in, you've satisfied that goal. The amount, it appears, is less important that the fact that the price for what the customer wants to buy, is reduced by his trade-in.

Don't be too hasty when making a deal. Don't let yourself drift into the same mental attitude as your customer. You must think of buying AND selling at a profit – making money on both ends of the deal. Plan carefully if you decide to take non-vehicle trades. Visit the local pawn shop, gun shop, jewelry store and used car lot. Talk to the owners. Explain that you're going to be taking everything and anything in trade. Offer to sell it to them if they're fair with you. You'll be surprised how many other business people will be only too happy to work with you.

When business is less than brisk and dollars are not floating as freely as you would like, consider the trade-in of anything of value as a potential for more sales and profit. Advertising that you take trades may be all that's needed to convert a would-be customer to a real buyer.

Points to remember:

1) Everything has a value.

2) Everyone wants a "deal."

3) Most people have something they no longer value.

4) Learn how to place a value on things.

5) Become a deal-maker.

Chapter 15

THE FOUR SEASONS

Selling powersports units and accessories is a four season business. It doesn't matter if you live in northern Minnesota or southern Florida, there are four distinct selling seasons – times of the year when different products and services are in demand. If you accept that fact (I can't conceive of why you wouldn't), then you must also know that your inventory must change to reflect each season.

Do you know what products or services relate to each season, and why? If you do know, are you doing anything about it? You should. On the next several pages I've listed the seasons and the products to which they relate. I also discuss the reasons these products should be highlighted.

Spring – Into Action

First, let's talk about spring (my favorite time of the year). Most riders store their bikes during the dead of winter – except for those in Southern California or the deep, deep south. The bikes are then rolled out on the first warm, sunny weekend. Spring is the time when the demand increases for batteries, tires, cables, carburetor cleaner and gasket sets, to name a few items.

We know that batteries should be charged and the water levels checked periodically, particularly if the bike is left unattended for several months. Few consumers remember to do it. The result: a dead battery. Depending on how long it has been dead, it may not come back to life with a simple charge. In humid climates throttle, clutch and brake cables may rust solid inside their housings. How many riders remembered to clean or lubricate the cables before storing the bike? None?

Gasoline, if allowed to age in carburetor float bowls, will evaporate over the long winter and leave behind a coating of shellac and plugged jets. Did the customer remember to drain the fuel system before storing the bike? You know he didn't. The fuel tank and filters will probably also need attention.

Just as people don't think of an umbrella on a sunny day, few riders think about their bikes until they're ready to ride. Then they come running to your store, usually in a panic, with a list of things they need ... right now!

SUMMER – VACATIONS

OK, spring's easy. What about summer? That's when touring riders look forward to traveling longer distances. The farther from home they expect to be the more important it is for them to be well equipped. Rainsuits, leathers, gloves, helmets, face shields, grips, tires, and repair kits are items you should have in stock before the summer months begin.

Think about the last time you used your rainsuit. Did you let it dry completely before you rolled it up? If you didn't, and you stored it in a dark place for three or more months, guess what it's going to look and smell like when you open the package. Mold seems to love to change yellow vinyl into sick green with splotches of black and gray. Tire repair kits and tank bags also sell well in the summer and should be in your stock.

FALL – OFF-ROAD

Fall has its own special considerations. Road activity usually diminishes except for some of the major national rallies. Off-road activity increases. Fall is a fashion show of the latest off-road apparel and accessories. In the ever-changing fashion end of competition products, NEW and IMPROVED riding gear which has been reviewed by the media creates a demand by those who must have the latest, trickest apparel or accessories. Young riders are very fashion conscious and look for these NEW rags.

WINTER – HIBERNATION

Winter lasts from three to seven months, depending on your geographical location. It's the put-it-away season. This is particularly true in the northern regions. Now you can sell that trickle charger, cycle cover, cleaners, lubricants and protective coatings. You may want to offer a booklet of suggestions on how to prepare your motorcycle for storage, along with a list of useful accessories. Some aggressive dealers offer to winterize and even provide the storage space for motorcycles. For a fee, of course.

Just when we've run out of seasons, here comes Christmas. There's an endless list of potential Christmas gifts. This special "season" used to last about 45 days. Today it lasts about two months. It starts slowly but finishes with a bang. Because of the special considerations the Christmas "season" offers, I won't attempt to cover the myriad of goods and services that come under the heading of Christmas specials.

Finally, when it's all over, you're into a new year. That's the time to make the internal changes you've been thinking about. You'll then be ready to face the spring once again.

Now that you've been so busy selling seasonal products, you'll have some time to take a vacation. That is if you don't have kids in school. February or March could be time for you to kick back for a while; you've earned it. Go ahead, have a great time. Of course, you may miss that early spring rush of riders who want to head south for Daytona Speed Week, and need tires or apparel – or maybe a helmet. Ah . . . well, you can't win 'em all.

Chapter 16

SELF-SERVICE

In a seller's market where demand exceeds supply, self-service works. When the items offered come under the heading of a commodity, self-service works. Self-service also works in businesses which employ clerks instead of knowledgeable sales people – places like K-Mart, Sam's Club, Wal-Mart, and most big box merchandisers. Self-service may become no-service if you attempt to use it as THE sales technique of preference in your powersports or accessory store.

Self-service is a very sophisticated business. It's not the same as just filling the shelves with products. Placement, color blocking, traffic patterns, POP (point of purchase) displays, and loss leaders, are all ingredients which contribute to a workable self-service program. The major mass merchandisers have made a science of self-service.

It's not just by chance that the $2.49 special on oil at K-Mart is all the way in the rear of the store. That was a conscious decision. Who buys $2.49 oil? K-Mart knows that the business executive doesn't. They know that the young family man – the man working his way up the business ladder – has a tight budget and needs to save money. They know that he works hard all week and does his own routine auto maintenance. They know he has kids at home. They know that when he sees the ad in the Saturday paper and decides to go to K-Mart to buy four quarts of $2.49 oil, he can't leave the house without the kids. K-Mart knows his wife has had the kids under her feet all week long and it's Dad's turn to take them.

When Dad gets to K-Mart with his two pre-school kids and heads for the $2.49 oil, what must he pass? K-Mart knows he has to pass the children's toy and clothing department. Have you ever tried to walk through the toy department with your kids? If you have you'll recognize these lines. "Daddy ... buy me this!" Daddy … I need one of these for school." "Daddy ... can I have ..." What loving Daddy can resist? By the time Daddy reaches the checkout counter with his four quarts of $2.49 oil, he has so much other stuff in the cart that the $60.00 he brought with him leaves him with less than $1.00 in change. Yes, K-Mart knows.

You don't have the options K-Mart does. You can't hire a store designer and a marketing expert to guide you. To be competitive your store should be a combination of self-service for commodity items and real-service for things that require information and decisions. You can't compete head-to-head with K-Mart. They have advertising and buying power beyond anything you'll ever experience. They can undersell you seven days a week and still make a profit.

Let's examine the difference between self-service and real-service as they relate to displays and sales people. Oil, chain spray, spark plugs, face shields, and the like, are commodities and lend themselves to self-service. Helmets, tires, apparel, chrome racks, suspension components and saddlebags, may be part of a mass display but are not self-service items. Don't confuse self-service with creative display. They may look the same but they require different levels of sales support.

A mistake some dealers make occurs after they remodel their stores. Now that they look like a mall store or a mass merchandiser, they believe that they are mysteriously converted into a self-service store, and that personal service is no longer required. They feel the store will do the selling without their help. The result? They put up a wall between themselves and their customers. The wall is often disguised as a parts counter. The "new" look of the store will generate incremental sales, at least for a while. But, as in all things, the "new" wears off sooner, or later.

Motorcycle parts and accessories lend themselves to dynamic displays. Salespeople who know how to stay out among these displays make things happen instead of just letting them happen.

A mirror will do no good unless the salesperson takes the customer by the arm and leads him to it to see how he looks with the helmet on, or in the jacket. The salesperson that stands with the customer to aid in the decision about which helmet or tire best suits his needs, will produce more dollars than one who lets the customer decide for himself, unaided.

Self-service is not total-service. Ours is a very complex industry. Our customers need our advice, opinions and counsel. They expect real service when making major purchases. We need repeat customers, not just people who come into our stores because we have a sale of $2.49 oil, but customers who value our knowledge and professionalism. We can't, and shouldn't try to compete with K-Mart. We're independent, entrepreneurial business people. We know we're dealing with enthusiasts to whom service is more than just a word. If we don't believe it, we're in real trouble.

Points to remember:

1) Self-service applies to commodities – not to product requiring careful decisions.

2) Self-service is too often very close to no-service.

3) Don't confuse mass displays of merchandise with self-service.

4) Big box merchandisers rely on self-service because few have qualified, knowledgeable salespeople.

5) Ours is a sophisticated industry requiring intensive guidance of the customer. Minimize self-service if you're interested in long-term profits.

Chapter 17

THE WORLD'S WORST SALESMAN

I've talked about it for years, but never thought it would happen to me. What am I alluding to? Coming face to face with the real-live example I've used for years when describing a bad salesman.

My overstated example was a stereotyped eclectic person made up of all the negative characteristics we've all encountered when we shop.
Was there such a being who embodied all those negative attributes? Deep down inside I was afraid there was.

I suppose it was only a matter of time before I met him. Finally, I did. For obvious reasons, I'll not divulge the name of the individual, nor the dealership. Things have changed for the better at this store, since I first wrote about it several years ago.

I was commissioned to do a marketing program for a very successful dealer. The owner met me at the airport early in the morning and drove me to the shop. On the way he suggested that I drop him off about a block away. He knew he had a sales problem but wanted me to see it for myself rather than describing it to me. He had taken the precaution of using his mother's car so it wouldn't be obvious I was driving the dealer's car.

I drove to the dealership and went in acting as an ordinary customer. There he was; his feet up on the desk, a cup of coffee in one hand a cigarette in the other. He was reading the morning paper. He was wearing a baseball cap, and never bothered to look up when he heard me come in.

I walked around the store for a few minutes, then went over to within 10 feet of him and sat on a bike. Now he looked up and spoke his first words. “Can I help you?”

I was tempted to say, “no thanks, just looking,” but that would be too easy. “Yes, I’m looking for a new touring bike. What does this one cost?” I asked, while sitting on a fully loaded tourer.

“About 18 thou,” was the curt reply. Then there was silence. The salesman returned to his paper, coffee and cigarette. The conversation stopped. I waited. Several long, agonizing minutes passed.

The salesman now rose slowly from his chair, cigarette still in one hand and coffee cup in the other. He walked toward me and sat on a nearby bike. It was obvious he had nothing more to say. If there was going to be any conversation, I’d have to initiate it.

“What about that one?” I asked, pointing to the bike next to him. “About the same,” he intoned.

It was not going well at all. OK, I thought, I’ll volunteer some information to get the conversation started again. “I used to own one of these about 10 years ago.” I said. “Have they changed much?”

“Yeah, they sure have.” The conversation died once again. Now I was starting to get angry. He just sat there drinking his coffee and blowing smoke in my face.

Finally, a sign of intelligence (small though it may have been). “What kind of riding do you do?” he asked.

“Mostly cross country touring,” I answered, hoping that now we would start communicating. “Well either one should do the job for you then,” he commented as he walked back to his desk. Again the conversation died. After what seemed to be minutes of uncomfortable silence, I said: “Thanks, I’ll just look around,” and wandered into the parts department. The “salesman” went back to his newspaper, coffee and cigarette.

I walked into the owner's office and flopped as dramatically as I could, into a chair. "This is going to be a tough one." I told the owner we had a lot of work to do. "That's why I wanted you to come here," he said.

No, this was not your run of the mill dealership. It was one of the top 20 dealers in the country for this franchise. They were doing a hell of a lot of business either by accident or in spite of themselves. If they decided to do business on purpose, there would be no limit to their growth.

In the past several years I have witnessed variations of this sales approach but never before had anyone done such a complete job of making it quite so hard for the customer to buy. No doubt about it, professionalism was not the byword of this store.

Attitudes were, to be generous, lousy. What was the salesman trying to prove? Why didn't he introduce himself or ask my name? Why didn't he try to qualify me? He could have asked questions; he didn't. He could have offered me a cup of coffee; he didn't. In short, he could have tried to sell me something; he never did.

This dealership had no after sale follow up. The internal systems and procedures were, for all practical purposes, nonexistent. But, the fact was that this particular dealer had out sold any other dealer in his geographical area. How? It wasn't low prices. Nor was it the general economy in the trading area. All I could conclude was that the demand was there. There were enough customers bent on buying to wade through the B.S. to get what they wanted.

This dealer was doing business by accident, and doing what would appear to be a good job. When I discussed things like hang-tags, yellow pages advertising, mirrors, and internal communications, I felt like I was rearranging the deck chairs on the Titanic. This dealership needed major surgery not minor cosmetic changes.

Then it struck me; this wasn't a business, it was a hobby. Everyone enjoyed the product; they were having fun. They had great technical expertise, and understood everything they needed to know about their brand of motorcycle. No one realized what the potential was, let alone how to achieve it.

This store could continue doing business as usual, and probably stay solvent for years to come. However, the OEM is aware of the market potential, and the diminishing market share for their brand. This store will have to change or face the prospect of having the OEM offer an additional franchise to someone else.

How many dealers are in this same dilemma? Are there many others who would rather just stay the same and not grow? How many more are experiencing "burn out?" I'm beginning to believe there are quite a few. My advice to them: Change your attitude or find someone to sell the business to while it still has a value.

Aggressive, organized, motivated, creative, retail powersports stores are exceptions. Although this event was extreme, I've encountered many others where selling motorcycles and other powersports units is a hobby. Unless and until the hobby attitude changes into a business attitude in stores like this one, the powersports industry will continue to slide in bad times and stagnate in good times.

This incident I've described happened several years ago. When I first wrote about it in *Dealernews* the owner called me. At first I expected him to be angry. He wasn't. He told me that the salesman was enrolled in a Dale Carnegie sales school, and that more changes were taking place. Since then the store has been remodeled, reorganized and revitalized. Sales of units, parts and accessories have increased more than 50 percent.

Chapter 18

THE ENTREPRENEUR

An entrepreneur is defined in Webster's as one who organizes, manages and assumes the risks of a business. An entrepreneur is also described as an aggressive businessperson; a motivated small business owner; a dynamic visionary; a winner.

Rarely is someone in the "big" corporate world called an entrepreneur. When someone fits the entrepreneur mold they are often called a rugged individualist and a self-made man.

Entrepreneurs are the business heroes of today. They are the role models fathers want their sons and daughters to emulate. Politicians now court their vote. It's considered un-American to say anything negative about this select category. Entrepreneurialism has never been as popular or received as much attention in the United States of America ... we're awash in 'em. I suspect a good number of the readers of this book count themselves among the ranks of this not so exclusive group of American Entrepreneurs.

There are three stages in the life of an entrepreneur. The achievement of the fist stage is easy to recognize and is celebrated by the business community. The business person who wears this title most often started from humble beginnings and established himself as the owner of a successful enterprise. All the positive aspects of guts, intuition, foresight, a strong work ethic, and the uncanny ability to see things more clearly than others, make up the ingredients of this unique, stage-one entrepreneur.

Major problems don't surface until the stage-one entrepreneur enters the second stage of development. Stage two can be, and often is, the downfall of the rising star.

As I've traveled the country, I've met many powersports dealers who have reached stage one and are justifiably proud. However, entering stage two many will succumb. Perhaps the title of this chapter should have been **"The Down Side of Entrepreneurship."**

As a small business grows, this special individual has the energy, awareness, and expertise to keep up with what's happening in each department. If he needs to, he can step in and do every job in the place and usually do it better than anyone else.

The entrepreneur has hand picked and trained each employee. Everyone is in awe of the boss's boundless energy and seeming ability to know everything. So far so good. However, as growth continues other skills are needed – skills not possessed by the entrepreneur who nonetheless attempts to operate outside of his expertise.

What is called for now is professional help. Disciplined, educated professionals must be consulted or hired. Authority and responsibility must be delegated and shared.

Fragile egos enter the picture. The entrepreneur has conceived, nurtured and developed his baby (the business), and as its creator, isn't anxious to have anyone else exercise even a modest amount of control over its growth and development.

The boss's authority will be challenged. Employees will begin to see him as a person with (for shame) faults. The god-like posture the entrepreneur has assumed will be viewed by formerly admiring subordinates, as part smarts and a larger part, luck.

Will the boss admit to not having all the answers? Is there a chance that he is making mistakes? Is the "baby" ready to grow up? I've found the answers to be no, no and: "Not until I say it's ready."

As more and larger problems surface blame must be placed, or at least spread around. The entrepreneur says, "I got us this far, if there's a problem you must have caused it. Now it's your problem so clean it up."

How do you recognize the entrepreneur among dealerships or accessory stores? Easy. He's the one cleaning the bathrooms because, "They just don't do it the way I want it done." He's the one who goes into the parts department, elbows aside the parts manager and negotiates with the warehouse rep directly. Then turning to the parts manager says: "See, that's the way to handle buying."

This is the person who knows exactly how the newspaper ad should look, and what it should say. Never mind that they have an advertising department or someone with talent in this area. The stage-two entrepreneur is easily recognized because he complains (or brags) that things just fall apart if he's not there every minute of every day. He "has not had a vacation in 12 years." In short, he's the one who just won't let go.

This stage-two entrepreneur will refuse to acknowledge that someone else has more relevant information or, God forbid, better ideas. They are the ones who suddenly become impatient because no one else thinks as fast as they do. They have, to date, refused to acknowledge they have any weaknesses or faults, although deep down inside they know that it just ain't so. Many have been living in fear of being found out.

If the entrepreneur can successfully negotiate this second stage, and not lose his sense of humor, the next stage will be easy. Stage three consists of letting other people make mistakes and learning from them. This is the stage when the entrepreneur can feel good about being smart enough to hire people better qualified than himself to do specific jobs. The entrepreneur can now sit back and do what he does best ... create.

Entrepreneurs are known to get bored once they're achieved their specific goals. They are anxious to go on to the next challenge. If properly guided by a caring staff, the entrepreneur can rise to new heights and become the leader of a team instead of an individual with carefully groomed clones.

To avoid the trauma and pitfalls of stage two, the entrepreneur should spend as much time as possible with other business owners who have moved into stage three. In doing so he can learn how to recognize many of the signs and behavior patterns that can threaten growth and development.

The one area in which the entrepreneur has the greatest problem is in learning how to relax, and let subordinates learn by making their own mistakes. The entrepreneur is by nature, a creative loaner. He must learn how to improve his communications skills, and learn how to show he too is human – and errs.

If you feel there's a possibility that you may be about to enter, or are in stage two, consider the following:

1) Take some time off.

2) Practice meditation or some other form of relaxation.

3) Talk to other business owners and friends about what you feel.

4) Admit to yourself and your subordinates that you're not perfect.

5) Ask for help.

Being an entrepreneur can be like being a millionaire; it's fun as long as you don't take yourself too seriously.

Chapter 19

THE PROFESSIONAL

In previous chapters I've repeatedly referred to professionals. You may well be a one. But are you sure? An annual theme, echoed by dealers at OEM new model introductions and other gatherings, is professionalism. Everyone seems convinced ... if they become more professional, success is sure to follow. When asked to describe professionalism, most come up with a vague or imprecise definition.

Being professional is more important today than it was 10 years ago because we're in a buyer's market and are dealing with better informed and often professional customers. Those among us who are pros will persist; those who are not, won't.

A definition in the dictionary describes the professional as a "calling requiring specialized knowledge and often long intensive academic preparation."

Lest you think all professionals must be college educated, let me assure you that's not the case. Going to college doesn't create professionalism. That condition follows education. Education may not necessarily mean institutional learning. We've all heard of the self-educated, successful person, and we've all met college educated turnips.

To understand professionalism we must first compare it to the alternative. The dictionary defines the antonym of a professional as an amateur, or novice. The most obvious comparison of the two conditions relate to sports. Professionals get paid; amateurs and novices don't. The same rule applies to the retail motorcycle business.

1) A professional is disciplined

He has taken the time to study his profession; that study never ends. The pro, for example, is reading this book and will read other books and articles in hopes of gaining useful information.

The amateur is not disciplined. The amateur will not read this book or any other designed to educate or inform him. He believes he already knows it all.

2) A professional attends seminars

He reduces his chances for blunders by studying, attending workshops and reading self improvement books and literature.

An amateur learns by making mistakes and (sometimes) adjusts as he goes along.

3) The professional attends industry shows and events

He attends the OEM shows, regional and national events like the Cincinnati Expo.

Amateurs stay home, convinced in their own minds that there's nothing to be learned or gained from attending such costly functions.

4) A professional accepts authority from other professionals

The pro realizes he isn't an expert on all subjects and looks to other professionals for help with marketing, accounting, or any area where he feels he can make substantive improvement.

The amateur seldom accepts authority other than his own, and feels intimidated by professionals even though their areas of expertise may be completely different.

5) The professional communicates with his competitors

A pro takes every opportunity to meet and discuss ideas with his competitors and fellow dealers. He encourages and attends as many dealer events as he can and exchanges ideas freely.

The amateur feels threatened by competition.

6) The professional alters his life-style to achieve his goals

Professionals know they must often set aside their personal lifestyles to pursue their careers. They are willing modify their behavior to achieve their goals.

Amateurs insist that others accept them as they are. They're not willing to make any adjustments in their lifestyles to achieve their goals – if they have goals.

7) A professional graciously accepts criticism

The pro accepts the fact he doesn't know-it-all and considers criticism part of his continuing education process.

An amateur takes criticism personally and becomes defensive. Amateurs are quick to defend themselves even when there's no cause to do so, that's because they are amateurs.

8) The professional looks like a pro

The pro dresses and acts in a practiced manner. It's no accident that lawyers wear three piece suits, doctors wear white coats, and ministers wear robes. The professional knows the world views him according to his appearance, as well as what he is qualified to do.

The amateur insists on "doing his thing," and dressing any way he likes. He resents having to conform. Conform is a dirty word to the amateur.

9) The professional's opinions are based on logic and evidence

The pro is willing to set aside his opinion if presented with facts contrary to those opinions.

The amateur may have strong opinions too, but stubbornly clings to his opinions and will defend them regardless of logic or the evidence.

10) A professional insists on evidence

The pro is unlikely to believe something just because someone told him it was fact. He weighs his own and other's opinions against facts.

An amateur believes in faith, not faith in the religious sense but faith defined as the superlative degree of gullibility.

11) The Professional knows there are no simple solutions

Professionals know there may well be a simple answer to a complicated problem, but they also know that there's a good chance that simple answer is wrong. The pro is willing to make long range choices only after considering all the options.

The amateur believes in simple solutions to complicated problems. I've heard one suggest that the manufacturers could solve all his problems by simply taking his (the amateur's) sage advice.

When I'm asked to speak to a group of professionals, it's often suggested that I'll be preaching to the converted. That may well be true. The professional considers attending these seminars and workshops part of being proficient. They are the converted. They've made the conversion from amateur to pro; a metamorphosis few make. We all start as amateurs. One in five of us has the ability to convert to the ranks of the professional – one in 20 makes it.

Professionalism is a relative degree. Pros always strive to improve. There's nothing relative about an amateur. An amateur is an amateur.

Therefore improvement is not a consideration to him unless he aspires to become a professional.

Professionals outlast amateurs in business. There will always be fewer of the former, and more of the latter. Changing from one to the other takes more concentrated effort than all but a select few are willing to endure. The 20/80 rule that says 20 percent of the dealers will do 80 percent of the business is, unfortunately what separates the pro from the amateur.

Based on the attributes I've described, do you feel you're a professional? If not, do you see how you can become one? In my view the answers to these questions is obvious. If you were an amateur you wouldn't have gotten this far in the book.

Chapter 20

THE MEETING

Or: How to have meetings, for people who hate meetings.

Why do we have to have meetings anyway? The answer is simple. The powersports retail business is complicated. It includes sales, service, financing, accounting, parts and accessories. In order to function smoothly all employees need to work as a team.

Individual and team goals must be understood. Progress must be measured. Corrections must be considered, and implemented. The only way to do these things is for everyone employed by the company to know what's happening, and what's expected of them. The way to accomplish that is by having all the employees meet to discuss goals. Employees feel more valued if their opinions are considered.

The spoken word is regarded as the weakest form of communications but the one we most often use. Oral communications between two people consist of approximately 500 different words; without the contractions. The problem is – according to Webster's dictionary – each word has an average of 18 definitions. Your chances of getting your idea across to someone else exactly the way you want to, is one out of 9,000 (18 definitions per word, times 500 words = 9,000). A communications expert may reduce those odds to, a still unacceptable, 1 in 2,000. Few store owners or employees are trained communicators – fewer are mind readers.

When I discuss meetings with a dealer, I can usually predict his reaction. "I hate meetings, they always end up as B.S. sessions." "Everyone gets their feelings hurt." "Meetings are a waste of time." "Nothing positive is ever accomplished by a meeting." "We're too busy to have meetings." Interesting isn't it, there always seems to be more reasons not to do something than to try it?

I believe the basic problem is not with the meeting but knowing how to run one. Regular weekly meetings can be productive, well run, and improve every part of your business from bookkeeping to ordering parts and accessories. The trick is setting up the ground rules and following them.

GROUND RULES FOR RUNNING A STAFF MEETING

1) Meetings must be no more than one half hour in length.

2) Meetings must be held before or after business hours.

3) Meetings are to be attended by **ALL** employees.

4) The meeting must be chaired by the manager or owner.

5) Everyone is to be encouraged to take an active part.

6) The chairman has the last word.

7) No one speaks without the chairman's permission.

8) Everyone must understand that meetings are business, NOT personal.

9) The goal of all meetings is improvement.

10) Each meeting must have an agenda.

Let's look at the format of a regular meeting. We'll assume that management does not have a specific agenda other than trying to improve the bottom line. Once the meeting is called, and everyone has his cup of coffee in hand, the chairman asks for problems.

Employees are encouraged to look for specific problems, not only in their areas, but anywhere they see one. (Business is solving problems. If there were no problems, there would be no business.) Once the problem is stated, the employee must offer what he feels is a reasonable solution.

Everyone is invited to talk about the solution, not the problem. The chairman appoints someone to take notes, or takes them himself. A plan of action must follow each meeting. The plan and follow-up report are presented at the next meeting.

Do these rules and steps seem easy? Sure they do, but that doesn't mean they'll be easy to put in practice. Someone much wiser than I, once asked, "If it's so easy why isn't everyone doing it?"

Personalities will come into play – that's to be expected. In order for people to work as a team they have to understand the personalities, strengths and weaknesses of the other team members. Without teamwork a company will flounder. Without regular meetings, there will be little teamwork.

What positive effects can you expect by conducting regular meetings? Employees will feel more a part of the company once they know its goals. Misunderstandings caused by weak communications skills will be replaced by appreciation of others' views. Acceptance of others' faults will encourage teamwork. There will be greater respect for management.

What can you expect if you opt to operate without constructive meetings? Improvement will prove to be elusive. Communications will continue to be iffy. There will be no team effort because there will be no team. Your store will be at the mercy of the general economy. In short, you'll have more of the same. If things are bad now … they'll get worse.

Go ahead, bite the bullet. Make an outline of what you want to happen and schedule your first meeting. Don't worry if things seem less than perfect. Start off by admitting you're not perfect and are looking for help. Let your staff know that each of you needs the other on his team.

Chapter 21

BUILDING AN "ABCD" TEAM

Teamwork is often talked about but not often practiced in the retail powersports business. When discussing team sports, as the name would imply, teamwork is the most important ingredient of winners.

To be a team player a person must forego his ego and instead of seeking individual recognition, learn to become part of the team. Few of us in the retail end of the motorcycle, watercraft, snowmobile or acces¬sory business understand how a team is built and why it's important.

In baseball, basketball, football or hockey, teamwork is built on specific skills of trained individuals. The same guidelines should apply to businesses. If teamwork is not practiced in your store, you may be placing square pegs (people) in round holes (the wrong job). The result? Winning, in the business sense, will elude you.

When I discuss building a company team with motorcycle dealers they give me the impression they consider the need for such a program to have a very low priority. Owners are seldom team players. Many feel that all they need are clones of themselves to have the perfect team. Nothing could be farther from the truth. When an owner sets out to hire people with behavioral tendencies and at¬titudes that match his, the results are often… disastrous.

There is little a person can do about his temperament or behavioral tendencies. These two aspects of the personality are genetic and environmental. With some effort, people who want to achieve specific goals can learn to modify their behavior to achieve those goals.

For simplicity's sake I've divided behavioral tendencies into four basic groups. Understanding which of the four best describes you will aid in understanding yourself and your fellow workers. This will lead to a more harmonious work place. In short, it can make your business more pleasurable.

It's difficult, some say impossible, to create a team if you don't know the player's talents and tendencies. Knowing will lead to understanding and team building. Of course, the team must have its captain (the boss), team leaders (managers), and team players (the staff). Each member must have a specific job description. However, if you want a winning team, the job descrip¬tion should fit the members' temperament.

Some dealerships and accessory stores I've visited have accidentally developed de-facto teams simply because the players have worked together so long that they've grown to understand each other, and have accepted the other person's behavioral tendencies and faults as being "just the way they are." This hit-or-miss approach is risky and can take a long time.

Problems will surface in a hit-or-miss team when a new player joins. This new member may be an employee who just came on board, or someone who's been transferred from one department to another. His acceptance by other members of the team may take months or even years. Sometimes the newcomer is never accepted.

Why not find a way to make the new player part of the team as soon as possible? If you do, you can create synergy: that condition where the sum of the parts is greater than the whole.

Behavior tendencies seldom surface until you've established a relationship in which that person feels confident enough to reveal himself. If people were able to determine each other's behavior tendencies as easily as they are able to define each other's physical characteris¬tics there wouldn't be nearly as many divorces or misun¬derstandings as there are today.

I've written 25 multiple choice questions designed to reveal your behavioral tendencies. Your answers to these questions will give you a peek into why you do what you do, and why people react to you the way they do.

If you can accept putting some labels on yourself, it will help.

People rejected labels back in the early '70s and have discarded so many that Mrs. was replaced with Ms. Without labels we find it difficult to identify things, or to call up mental images. Labels help us to be more accepting if we can identify objects or attitudes by name. People, places, and yes, even attitudes and tendencies are easier to deal with if they have labels (names).

So you won't feel bad about yourself, I've given these labels non-threatening names; calling them simply A, B, C, and D tendencies. There's no right or wrong within these categories – just as there's no right or wrong, good or bad, when it comes to things you like or don't like. There are only preferences, proclivities, priorities, temperaments and tendencies.

This little test does not purport to be a definitive probe into your personality make-up. It was designed to give you a broad overview of yourself. Do be careful that you don't take this too seriously. Use it only as a guide. It's not the gospel according to St. John.

First, let your mind go blank. Don't think about the answers. Don't try to second guess. No one is going to see the results but you. Then read the question and then quickly circle the appropriate letter under the headings of: NO, ?, OK, and YES.

If you believe the statement does not apply to you circle the letter under the word "NO." If you're ambivalent, circle the letter under "?".

Does the statement somewhat fit you? If so, circle the letter under "OK." If the statement is one with which you agree, circle the letter under "YES."

Next, total each letter and put the number next to the appropriate letter on the "Total" line. If all the numbers are within one or two of each other that's fine. It suggests you may not have to modify your behavior unless your job requirements call for a par¬ticular set of tendencies. If you have a very high number after one letter and smaller numbers under the others, you have a stronger behavioral tendency.

Neither case is bad. If your numbers are spread out evenly you can probably fit well in any job your company wants you to do. On the other hand, if you scored very high in one category it would be best to consider an occupation where that particular pattern of behavior would be best used.

OK, take the test on the following page.

ABCD - BEHIVIOR TENDENCY EVALUATION

	NO	?	OK	YES
1. I'm very confident in my ability.	A	B	C	D
2. I speak well and can dominate conversations.	A	B	C	D
3. I am very knowledgeable in my area.	B	A	D	C
4. I make friends easily and quickly.	C	D	B	A
5. I'm a careful and detail oriented person.	A	B	C	D
6. I have a strong feeling of self worth.	A	B	C	D
7. I follow up and keep my promises.	B	A	C	D
8. I use facts and figures to make my point.	A	B	D	C
9. I'm very enthusiastic and animated.	C	D	B	A
10. I enjoy learning and telling jokes.	C	A	B	D
11. I have trouble getting started mornings.	B	D	A	C
12. I'm a very good listener.	C	D	B	A
13. I get upset when people lie to me.	B	A	D	C
14. My feelings are easily hurt.	C	D	A	B
15. I get impatient when people are slow deciding.	A	B	D	C
16. If I don't know the answer I may bluff.	B	C	A	D
17. Other people consider me an expert.	A	B	D	C
18. I often forget a promise.	C	D	B	A
19. I consider myself to be very ambitious.	B	A	C	D
20. I'm easily bored.	C	D	A	B
21. I'm considerate if I disagree with someone.	B	C	A	D
22. I'm very organized and on time.	B	A	D	C
23. New ideas and things excite me.	C	A	B	D
24. I ask a lot of questions.	C	D	A	B
25. I have a tendency to talk more than listen.	A	B	C	D

TOTAL: A: ______ B: ______ C: ______ D: ______

Add up your point totals for each letter you circled. The letter with the highest point total can be considered as your more prominent behavioral tendency.

BEHAVIOR TENDENCIES PERSONAL PROFILE

OK, let's assess the results of your profile test. Pick the letter – A,B,C or D – for which you had the highest point total. Assess your personality tendencies below to see what roles you may be well suited for... and therefore are likely to be the most successful in.

A-Behavior

AMIABLE – EASY GOING AND UNDERSTANDING – NOT TECHNICAL – FAIR SELF-CONFIDENCE – ENTHUSIASTIC – THINKS ON HIS FEET – GOOD LISTENERS

Wants personal recognition - Not interested in details - Enthusiastic - If in selling may oversell - Too wordy - Considers objections to be personal - Tends to ramble

Best jobs: Sales - Service writers
Worst jobs: Parts department - Mechanic - Accounting

B-Behavior

BENEFACTOR – SUPPORTIVE OF FELLOW EMPLOYEES – GOOD AT MEDIATION – MEDIUM SELF-CONFIDENCE – VERY LIKEABLE PERSON – FRIENDLY – FAMILY ORIENTED

A natural salesman but doesn't know it - Likes to be prepared - May be repetitive with information - Lacks animation - May feel offended by resistance - Spends time on minor points and may not address major problems

Best jobs: Store managers - Service managers
Worst jobs: Buyers - Accounting - Parts managers

C-Behavior

CALCULATING – THESE ARE NUMBERS PEOPLE – HIGH SELF-CONFIDENCE IF SUPPORTED BY DOCUMENTS – GOOD FOLLOW THROUGH

The pragmatists - Not very understanding of weaknesses of others - Deals with facts, not opinions - Make decisions based on evidence - May over-use statistics - Gives too much data - Has high standards but shows little emotion - Some products and people may be beneath his standards

Best jobs: Accounting - Parts sales - Buyers
Worst jobs: Unit sales - Store managers

D-Behavior

DETERMINED AND AGGRESSIVE – LIKES TO SELL BUT NOT SERVICE – ONLY COMFORTABLE IF HE IS IN CONTROL – STRONG EGO AND HIGH SELF-CONFIDENCE – GOOD TALKER

Confident but often unprepared - Does not concentrate on listening - Tends to dominate conversations - May try to steamroller even small objections - When challenged tends to over-react - Has ability to control his mood and attitude

Best jobs: Sales - Advertising depart¬ment
Worst jobs: Accounting - Buyers - Mechanics

Chapter 22

CHANGING TIMES

During the ‘80s and ‘90s most retail powersports stores were open five days a week. In some parts of the country the store was closed on Monday, in other parts, Wednesday. Few stores were ever open on a Sunday. The rationale I heard from the dealers was that if you couldn’t be profitable working five days a week you were doing something wrong. They argued that their employees needed two days off and by being closed on Sunday and Monday they could have that time to be with their families and enjoy themselves. In Georgia, I discovered, Wednesday was a traditional “going fishing day.”

Today a store’s open schedule is changing more rapidly than any other single event.

Although they are rapidly declining, some states still have blue laws in place mandating that neither motorcycles nor automobiles can be sold on a Sunday. Some of these same states also prohibit the sale of alcoholic beverages on Sundays too. I suppose these laws were put on the books about 100 years ago and no one has thought of changing them.

I remember back when I lived in Georgia, the “conventional” wisdom was that the preachers and the moon-shine producers would both stagger to the polls and vote “dry.” While there are still some more or less dry states, it appears to be those which have de facto state religions. The prohibition of Sunday retailing is slowly going away, however, as those states begin to understand that they too need more sales taxes to support themselves. The economy will often take precedence over unpopular and vague religious concerns.

Today, thanks to companies like Wal-Mart, K-Mart and Sears, most big box retailers are open seven-days a week and many boast of being open 24 hours a day. Their mix of products covers everything from automotive needs to grocery and leisure activity products.

Why the change in retailing? The economy and the lifestyles of Americans have changed. Religious prohibitions are being pushed off the table as the retailers begin to realize that many of their customers work five days a week and are reluctant to take time off from work to shop. The economy has also forced retailers to seek more ways to entice customers to shop in their stores. What better way than to make them so convenient that the customer can come to the store whenever he or she feels the urge to shop?

The Internet has proven that we are in a 24/7 economy. Now the need for market share has done about the same thing. This time, too, Harley-Davidson dealers seem to be taking the lead.

If you go on the Internet and check on the store hours of Harley-Davidson dealers you'll discover that most are now open all seven days. Yes, there are some that have rather convoluted hours like open 10 am to 7 pm on Monday and Wednesdays; 9 am to 8 pm Tuesday and Friday; 9 am until 6 pm on Saturday and 10 am to 4 pm on Sunday. I believe that, too, will soon go away as dealers discover anything other than "mall" hours confuses the consumer. What are mall hours? They are 10 am until 9 pm, Monday through Saturday and 10 am to 6 pm on Sunday.

Progressive dealers are aware that market share will be the name of the game. They are adding and shifting their hours in the hope that they'll attract more customers. Those who have are reporting some surprising results. For example, I talked to Gary Harper the Chief Operating Officer for Cycle Barn in Lynwood, Washington. Jim Boltz, the store's owner and I have argued for years about store hours. Jim was adamant about staying the course and operating no more than five days a week. One of Gary's first major challenges was to change from a five-day store to a seven-day one.

Did it make any difference? I called Gary and here's what he told me: "The first Sunday we were open we sold about $25,000 in part and accessories. That surprised us because we didn't think the consumers would know of the change in store hours." Obviously, many did.

Why did Gary take this dramatic step particularly considering that the store's owner was not inclined to support the change? He knew that some of his competitors were contemplating changing their hours too.

For those geography challenged (how's that for political correctness), Lynwood is a suburb of Seattle, Washington. Boeing and Microsoft are two of the largest employers in the state. Both have been downsizing due to the shifting economy. It has had a profoundly negative effect on the overall economy of Seattle.

People who are out of work are reluctant to obligate themselves by buying a bike; however, those who still have jobs and want to buy are reluctant to take time off work to do so. Now that this, and I suspect, more stores in the Seattle area, will be open both more days and longer hours the result will be more sales, higher CSI, and more long-term and loyal customers.

OK, so Cycle Barn's decision to open seven days a week seems to make sense based on the economy of the area but what about Albuquerque, New Mexico? There is little unemployment there, the economy is very stable thanks to companies like Intel, the Sandia labs and tourism along with a home building boom, so one would wonder, why be open seven days a week here? No other franchised store is open on Sunday; one is closed both Sunday and Monday. Again, the Harley-Davidson dealership run by Chick Hancock has moved the bar. Chick too has opted to be open seven days a week. Why?

I stopped in to visit and asked. His response: "We often have events that start at our store on Sunday morning. We noticed people we've never seen before coming in and looking around. So, after much hard negotiating with the employees we decided to open the store from 11 am to 4 pm on Sunday. What we've discovered is there is a rather large segment of potential buyers who would or could not visit us during our regular hours but love to come in and shop on Sunday. I don't believe we're cannibalizing our own existing customers but adding new ones.

We're quite happy with the turnout and expect it to increase as the word gets around." Eric Dayhoff, Chick's sales manager, confirmed that there were many new people never seen at the store in the past. "We stayed busy from the time we opened until the time we closed each Sunday, regardless of the weather. We expect to see Sundays as our number two or three strongest sales days of the week."

Both Chick and Eric concluded that the retail business mandates Sunday hours if growth and stability are concerns. They also admit that it's quite a selling job to get the staff on board. However, once it was explained that no one was being asked to work more than five days a week and that most employees could anticipate two consecutive days off it solved the problem.

Will this paradigm spread to other brands? It already has. I suspect that in the near future we'll see "open seven-days-a-week" signs on many more store windows.

Chapter 23

DIVERSIFY OR DIE?

I confess . . . I'm the one who wrote the article entitled "Diversify or Die." It was published by *Dealernews* many years ago. The piece appeared about the time our industry was entering its steepest decline in 20 years. Since then things have changed. Business and profits are better for many retailers. Because truth is a function of time, I'd like to reexamine diversification options.

The OEMs began the move toward true diversification when they introduced power products, watercraft, lawn care machinery, snowmobiles, and utility vehicles, all carrying their familiar motorcycle logos. Many (but not all) of their dealers were offered the new lines. These diversified products have proven to be the salvation for a number of large dealers – those whose cost of operation mandate a substantial cash flow.

The total number of dealers in the country has declined (a condition I believe is not all bad). Many of those who are left have found it necessary to consider diversification to assure continued growth. Today there's a myriad of opportunities to diversify. One being considered by a large contingent of dealers is adding another line of motorcycles.

At several OEM new model introductions recently, I was asked by literally dozens of dealers, for my opinion about adding another brand of motorcycle. Most asked because they were timorous about "putting all our eggs in one basket." The motivation repeatedly put forward for adding another line was the belief that even though the dealer felt he had shown his loyalty to a company whose marquee is displayed on the gas tank, he was less than comfortable with the OEM's allegiance to him. Historically that contention has been proven valid in many instances.

The prospect of adding another brand of bikes is a seductive one. It's challenging to use your expertise to re-establish a name in your market after a long absence, or after being poorly represented. Then too, you may feel if you don't take on the line someone else will, creating a new competitor.

If you have been approached by an OEM, or are considering adding a line of bikes, please weigh the following arguments before making your final decision.

If you have one franchise and add another will your sales double? Unlikely. Sales of parts may increase. You may have a modest growth of unit sales but you may be simply transferring sales from one brand of motorcycle to the other.

You will, however, double your inventory of parts and perhaps units. You'll need more special tools, signs and forms.

Once you have two competing lines, you will have to find a way to answer a customer who asks, "which is better?" The additional franchise will mean you'll have to send your mechanics out for more schooling. You'll need additional showroom space, more advertising, and other costly requirements demanded by the "new" commitment.

Once you've weighed these elements you may well opt to add the line, providing you have the necessary cash and credit to do so. If that's your pragmatic business decision, go for it and good luck! If your decision was an emotional one, take care. I've talked to more dealers who, in retrospect, have regretted adding a line than those who felt it was a good decision.

What are your alternatives to adding another brand while protecting your investment and continuing to show personal financial growth? Assuming you have some cash and credit (You must have, else why would you be considering adding another line?), why not invest in another business? No, I'm not suggesting you diversify YOUR motorcycle business ... I'm recommending you invest in a different business enterprise as a silent or inactive partner.

There are literally thousands of small businesses run by ambitious, enthusiastic people who are undercapitalized and handicapped by a lack of management experience or guidance. If your motorcycle store is successful and you have enough capital and spare time, your management skills along with an infusion of cash or credit may be just the elements needed to assure some other company will prosper. Your reward will be to share in that prosperity.

Think back to the time you started your dealership. Wouldn't it have been great if someone offered you both capital and management training? Would you have been willing to share the profits with that person? Would taking in an investor have accelerated your growth or added more dollars to your bank account?

Of course, we'll never know the answers to those questions, or the questions about your willingness or ability to work with a new partner with, perhaps, a different personality, priorities and work ethic.

If you're not interested in getting involved in a different occupation or adding another brand of bike, consider this option: Invest in inventory that will generate a higher percentage of return on investment than new motorcycles; products like used motorcycles, used watercraft, accessories and parts. This option will give you the flexibility and freedom to control your own destiny without involving the OEM in your marketing decisions.

It will require the least amount of cash and will not adversely impact your ability to concentrate on your existing enterprise. You won't have to start at the bottom of a learning curve mandated when developing new relationships and learning the language of another business.

Do you ***need*** to diversify outside of your existing business? Would a higher level of involvement in your current business show a return? How willing are you to invest not just the time but the energy necessary to assure some degree of success in a totally new endeavor?

Contrary to common belief, the grass is not necessarily greener on the other side of the fence. Of course, it will be greener over the septic tank, to borrow from Erma Bombeck.

Options to consider if contemplating diversifying your business:

1) Do you have the capital to add a new product line?

2) Do you have, and are you willing to dedicate the necessary space?

3) Can you spare a staff member(s) for off-site training?

4) How steep is the learning curve and how long before you can expect a profit?

5) Are you enthusiastic about the new direction you're about to take?

6) What are the downsides?

7) Do you feel you've exhausted your market for your existing lines?

8) Is your decision based on emotional or pragmatic reasons?

Chapter 24

ACTIVITY AND INVOLVEMENT

Anyone who has ever sat through one of my seminars knows how I've pounded on this subject for years. Nothing, in my opinion, will have as much of an influence on sales as the involvement with the consumer in off-premises activity.

OEM and accessory manufacturers claim that involvement with the end user is their best way to stay informed, plan future products, get ideas for improvement, and claim a greater market share. Every company has its own priorities and level of involvement. However, the greater the involvement, the greater the reward. Dealers must adopt a similar attitude and become involved with their customers.

When the owners of Harley-Davidson took the company public the stock was offered at $11, if memory serves. Most of the large brokerage firms issued a "no-buy" recommendation to their clients. While I don't claim to know the reasons, I can speculate that the brokers looked at the motorcycle market and saw it was in a steep decline at the time. They may also have looked at Harley-Davidson's product line and determined that Harleys were not as technically advanced as the imports. The stock sank to about $7. Then the stock started its dramatic rise, confounding the brokers, who could see no apparent reason.

A few years after Harley went public one of the brokerage firms discovered their secret; the HOG club. This discovery prompted one broker I know to comment: "The HOG club is as close to a license to steal as I've ever seen. It was a stroke of genius for Harley to come up with that idea. I wish I'd invested in the company myself." The HOG club has become the best marketing tool available to Harley dealers. Why? It forces activity and involvement.

As I travel the country visiting dealers I've discovered only one common thread separating those who are up-beat and see a bright future from those who are depressed and see no light at the end of the tunnel. That common thread is the dealer's involvement in activity with the end user (their customers).

Dealers who sponsor rides, rallies, races, seminars and other fun events have good floor traffic which relates directly to good cash flow. Dealers who dismiss the idea because they feel it's too much trouble, or not worth their time, suffer the consequences of lost potential. At least part of the growth in Harley's market share, I'm convinced, is directly related to the HOG club activity. Dealers who are involved with the **Harley Owners Group** support my contention.

Motorcycling is an enthusiast's sport. Although it is most often a solo activity, riding with a group has its special rewards. When anyone adopts a hobby, and motorcycling is in all but a few isolated cases, a hobby, the first thing they want to do is meet other people with whom they can share their interest. The reward is expanding their circle of friends. In the parlance of the "New Age" people, these motorcyclists are enlarging their support group.

The American social patterns are changing. People are spending less time watching TV, a condition that has the networks terrified. Instead of sitting in front of the tube getting stupid, they're joining churches, associations and clubs. Conversation, which all but disappeared in the late '70s and early '80s, is returning as a viable alternative to non-participating activities.

A major reward to being part of a club, as expressed by the participants of a variety of motorcycle organizations, is more than just riding together – it's talking to each other at rest stops, restaurants, race tracks, and wherever they gather when not in the saddle. Lasting friendships are spawned based solely on the one common denominator: they enjoy motorcycles.

Literally millions of dollars have been willingly given to deserving charities by motorcycle clubs whose participants are happy to pay for the privilege of riding with people whose company they enjoy. Dealers have become local heroes and received front-page publicity when they involve themselves in worthy causes along with their customers.

Several years ago my seminar theme was, "Get Involved or Get Out." There are still a few dealers who refuse to get involved but most have already gotten out – all but a few, involuntarily. We are in an enthusiast's sport. Our customers expect us to be enthusiasts too. They want to be involved with us socially. That means we have to ride with them on the weekends, which is the only time they have to ride; they work all week.

Is the motorcycle retail business any different from any other enthusiast retail business as it relates user activity? Is it any different, for example, from the gun shop, ski shop, diving shop, bicycle store or hang glider retailer? I don't think so. Sure, there are non-involved mass merchandisers and corporate stores that sell a variety of sports and enthusiast products. But once the customer gets serious and changes from a casual user to an active hobbyist, his allegiance and source of information moves to the enthusiast, independent, entrepreneur: YOU.

Disagree if you will, and there are many who do, but it is my opinion that if you don't get involved your chance for success in today's market is less than fifty percent of that of an involved dealer.

How do you get involved considering you're very busy? Simple. I'll bet you have at least one regular customer who is an active leader and appears to have an entourage who follow him around. Call him aside and ask him to start the club for you. Explain that because of your work schedule you can't be as actively involved as you would like. Offer to take care of the mailings and volunteer your store as a meeting place. Suggest rides which benefit specific recognized charities. Be prepared to spend a little money on door prizes. Become the seat of motorcycle activity in your market.

Years ago, I visited with a Mr. R. E. Miller, a Kawasaki dealer in South Africa. Every weekend the store hosted a ride. Over the years it became so popular that upwards of 2,000 motorcycles gathered at the shop each Sunday morning, rain or shine. Mr. Miller told me he sold more motorcycles and accessories on Sundays than all the rest of the weekdays combined.

It's a terrible statistic, but I've discovered one third of the owners of motorcycles over 750cc ride less than 1,500 miles per year. Folks, that ain't good news. Imagine walking past the bike parked in the garage with only a few thousand miles on the clock. How long do you suspect the owner will do that before he decides to trade the bike in, not on another motorcycle but on a bass boat, computer or truck? How many tires, batteries or other accessories are you going to sell to someone who rides so seldom, or such short distances?

It's up to you. No one else is going to encourage owners to ride. Activity is directly related to sales. There are parts of the country which boast of literally hundreds of events a year. The dealers tell me that most of these events are well attended. How do they know? They attend! They're not complaining; they get involved.

Events like those, which take place in Sturgis, Laconia, Daytona, Leguna Seca, and Lake George (the Americade) grow every year. Why would that be happening if the riders weren't interested in the activity and involvement?

Motorcycles are not commodities; they're high-priced toys for big boys (and girls). Give the boys and girls a way to play with their toys and they'll soon wear them out, want to change them, personalize them, or buy more of the same.

Chapter 25

SECURITY & CROOKS

Chains and small padlocks offer security to valuable leather and textile apparel at all too many dealerships. Besides offering security, they also inhibit the customer who may want to try on, and buy, a jacket. When asked why such extensive measures are considered necessary, most dealers will allude to the crime rate in their neighborhood.

Some dealers have iron bars on their front windows or elaborate security systems connected to monitoring stations. Then, in the middle of the night, the dealer's or general manager's sleep is interrupted by a call from the police who report that someone drove a truck through the front window and loaded up several new motorcycles along with a complete ensemble of wearing apparel, helmets and spare parts. No, they have not a clue as to who the perpetrators were. No, you'll never see your goods again.

Unfortunately, this problem is not just a nighttime thing. More than one dealer has told me of customers coming in the store and walking out wearing a new leather jacket or helmet. However, the most unusual case I heard was told to me by Don Tilley, a Harley-Davidson dealer in Statesville, North Carolina.

Don's store was robbed one night. The thieves left with a pickup load of leathers. The next day several jackets were found at a nearby trailer park. The police were called in. A search of the area turned up two teen-age boys with several new Harley leather jackets. However, because there was no way to prove the leathers were stolen from Don's store and the thieves didn't confess, they were allowed to keep the jackets.

Is there anything you can do to protect yourself from thieves? I'm sad to say there is for all practical purposes no real defense against a professional crook. If a pro is intent on robbing you, there's little you can do to stop him.

And today's crooks are more professional than ever. Armed with high tech criminal tools, and working under cover of darkness and driving a stolen vehicle, a drug-using, desperate, armed thief will, nine times out of ten, get away with your goods. They'll shoot or poison your dog, cut the phone and power lines to your store and may even shoot you if you try to stop them. You had best have a good insurance policy and at least the appearance of being concerned about your security.

I was first made aware of the security problem while visiting with a group of dealers. Two of the dealers had been approached by a company selling some very high tech security devices. The dealers asked me if I knew anything about these things. I knew very little of the fancy electronic pieces the literature described. However, the five figure price tag was easy to see. "Is it worth it?" A dealer asked. I couldn't, in all honesty, recommend the dealer shell out that amount of money based on my knowledge.

The question of security began to haunt me. I did a little research and talked to a few insurance companies and security equipment manufacturers and dealers. What I learned could best be called common sense. (Funny, they call it common sense, when it's uncommon sense.) Here's what was related to me.

The perception that you have good security will outweigh the reality. Some examples of what this means are as follows:

Reducing Thefts That Take Place While You're Open

1) Mirrors

Have large mirrors strategically placed in as many areas of your showroom as possible. Even though they don't work very well, have one, or several, of those large convex mirrors fastened to the ceiling or wall.

Rationale: Crooks don't want to be caught. Most often they look around before they steal. If they see mirrors they feel insecure and will probably opt to try another shop.

2) Traffic Control

Have a checkout counter or some method of controlling traffic near the front door.

Rationale: A thief doesn't want you too close to him when he's about to leave with stolen goods. You might recognize your products.

3) Special Markings

Use a special mark on your high-ticket items. If it's clothing, use an odd shaped hole punch and make a small hole in the tag inside the garment. When you sell the garment punch another hole. If this had been done in Don Tilley's store, he may have gotten at least some of his leathers back.

Rationale: If you suspect someone has tried on some apparel and is about to walk out with it, there will be little you can do if you have no proof that the garment is yours. The thief will just claim he came into your store wearing it. If there's no hole punched in the tag, he didn't get if from you. If there's one hole punched, you can show the police how you identify your inventory. If there's two holes punched, you've sold it and although it may have been stolen it happened after you sold it.

4) Security Tags

Buy plastic security tags and fasten them to the straps on the helmets and the zip pulls on the garments even if you don't have the electronic security device that is triggered when the plastic tags pass between them.

Rationale: Just as the dummy TV cameras and signs that say the premises are protected by the XXX SECURITY CO. have a chilling effect on a would be thief, so do the plastic tags. The thief doesn't know there's no machine to thwart him.

5) Mingle

Get out from behind the counter and mingle on the sales floor.

Rationale: You have a better opportunity to make sales ... and a thief is not left alone to see how he can rip you off. This is very important where accessories are on gondolas, which limit the ability of the salesperson to see what a customer is doing.

6) Prosecute

If someone is caught stealing from you, prosecute them.

Rationale: Thieves stick together. If they find out you are a pushover, you can expect to have more thieves coming through your doors. Their risk of getting caught is lessened by the belief that you won't follow through with a formal complaint.

Reducing Thefts That Tale Place When You're Closed

1) Security Lights

Leave one bright light on in each area inside and outside the store. Good lighting does make a difference.

Rationale: Thieves don't like to work within the spotlight.

2) Security Sign

Have a sign outside the store stating that you have a security system and will prosecute offenders.

Rationale: The thief feels the pressure of additional risks.

3) Walk Around

Take a trip around your building at least once a week and try to think like a crook. Check the dumpster.

Rationale: Often a dishonest employee will dump something in the trash, then come back at night and retrieve it. Someone planning to break in will frequently leave his tools at the site before the robbery.

4) Police Help

Tell the police you'd like them to drive by and shine their light in your store as often as they can. Let them know you feel less than secure. Don't worry about appearing paranoid; it's your investment you're protecting.

Rationale: If the police are put on the alert, they do respond; it's their job!

5) Neighborhood Watch

Just as there are neighborhood watches for residential areas, consider establishing one with your business neighbors.

Rationale: A thief who steals from one retailer most often stays in the neighborhood and steals from others. If there's a suspicious character about, you can warn each other.

There are a myriad of other measures designed to help you protect yourself. Especially in today's market where high tech security solutions abound – and security companies would like nothing better than to make you part with your hard-earned money on their solutions.

You must accept that you will have some potential for losses due to thieves. Don't let that potential curb your chances for sales by appearing to be paranoid to your customer.

Chapter 26

COMMUNICATIONS HIT RATE

"The spoken word is
the poorest form of communications known to man."

I don't know who said it first, but I agree with the person who said it. Your hit rate (the number of sales per customer contact), can be vastly improved if you learn the art of clear communications.

According to those who study and report on such things, verbal communication has the dubious honor of accounting for about 10 percent of all communication between people. The remaining 90 percent or so consists of eye contact, gestures, body language, and touch, to name the most important ones.

To further compound the problem, those same researchers I've alluded to above, say there is an average of 18 definitions per word. Just think, how may different meanings there are to the word: spoke, tank or even tire? The definition of some words changes with changing values and times. "Hot pants" has had completely different meanings over the years. So have expressions like "bad" and "gnarly."

The following story illustrates just how difficult communications can be, even for a mother and her daughter.

A little girl came home from school and asked her mother the meaning of the word "vice." The shocked mother felt that if her little girl wanted to know, it was her duty to explain. So she told her daughter about drinking, gambling, drugs and other vices. Her daughter sat there wide-eyed. When she was finished with the explanation, the mother asked her daughter why she wanted to know. The little girl responded: "I was just elected VICE President of my class and I wondered what it meant."

No wonder there is so much misunderstanding when two people, who have never met before, try to hold a conversation for the first time. When they first attempt to communicate with each other and discover they don't share the same level of understanding, or speak each other's unique jargon the chances of communicating feelings, opinions or ideas, between them diminishes exponentially.

If you and whomever you are attempting to relate to are about the same age, have similar education and life experiences, and come from the same religious, ethnic and geographical backgrounds, you have a fair chance of establishing an acceptable level of communication. That level will improve over time as each gets to know the other's unique qualities.

That's fine if the event is a casual or personal encounter, but what happens if you have an agenda? What can you expect if, for example, you're trying to sell something to someone you've just met? You'd best hone your communications skills or risk repeated rejections and failures resulting in depression.

Short of going back to school to study communications or improving your vocabulary, there is, I believe, no quick fix. Because of the constant change in our market new people with poor communications skills have replaced many of the "old timers" with better-developed skills. Many of today's young counter salespeople and unit sales staffs are intimidated by mature and better informed customers, making communications still more difficult.

Few of the young salespeople have had sales training, let alone training to improve communications skills. Sales practice time is rarely set aside and few owners or managers have taken it upon themselves to insist, or demand, these less-than-tangible activities be incorporated into their operations manual or business training priorities.

It's easy to re-do the store; re-paint the floor; re-arrange the inventory; try new and exciting marketing and print ads; and increase the general dealership activity. But there is nothing that will improve the bottom line more than improved communications skills.

There is one suggestion that I feel offers a potential shortcut and perhaps a way to bypass some of the more serious problems caused by undeveloped skills; one simple change in your operation that could do wonders for your bottom line. That shortcut is...asking questions and waiting for the answers.

Sounds simple doesn't it? It is. Then why do so few new sales people practice it? The answer to that question escapes me. Perhaps you have a clue, I don't. I could conjecture that a poorly informed salesman is afraid to ask questions for fear he wouldn't know what to do with the answers. Product knowledge and practice will help reduce the communications gap, if my supposition is valid.

Would you like to see if this shortcut works and have some good-natured fun? After you've finished reading this chapter, start a conversation with a fellow employee. Don't make any statements ... ask questions. Try to discover some personal thing about your fellow worker's eating habits, for example. Or something else you don't know. Then ask questions until your cohort discovers what you're doing.

The next step? Give him the book with the suggestion he read this chapter.

You've just improved your communications skills. Congratulations!

Chapter 27

OVERCOMING "NO"

When I travel around conducting my seminars on sales and marketing, I know that only a small percentage of the information I pass along will be remembered. I know, for example the audience will remember about 10 percent of what I tell them and their minds will drift away about every 20 seconds. Therefore, it's important to me that the participants take away at least one strong message. That message relates to the title of this chapter. Simply put, that message is: **Never Ask A Question That Can Be Answered With A Simple "No!"**

Why is this point so important? Think about it for a moment. Yes or no answers reveal little about how a customer feels or what he thinks. The word **NO** is a powerful negative.

For example, if you ask, "May I help you?" the answer is, nine out of ten times, "No thanks, just looking." Once the customer has said "NO" the conversation has ended. To make matters worse, the customer is now in charge of the conversation. What happens next? Just as you're walking away after receiving the "NO" answer, the customer turns and asks you a question. Now you have to turn around, walk back and then wait until you're asked another question. The customer is pulling your string. He's in charge of what's happening, not you. He feels the power and knows, perhaps subconsciously, he's in charge.

When the first word a customer utters is NO, it's then easier for him to continue to say NO to anything else you ask. What type of questions should you ask? You should ask questions to gain information – questions phrased in such a way that the customer gets the chance to express himself – to tell you how he feels about something.

Children are often inhibited when talking to strangers. Because of their caution they prefer to either answer questions with one word or simply nod their heads. How many interviews have you seen where the interviewer carefully asks questions a child can answer yes or no? That same child will ask questions to get information. Rarely will a child ask simple yes or no questions. Children like to get information. They want to learn; that's why they ask so many questions. They also want to be in control. Sometime during their formal education this condition changes, for what reason I'll never know. That it does change is regrettable.

It will take practice to develop the habit of asking questions to gain information while staying in control. You might start that exercise at home. If, for example, you want to go out to dinner don't ask your wife if she would like to dine out. Instead say: "Let's eat out tonight. Would you rather go to the Chinese restaurant, or would you prefer the Italian place?"

In some parts of the country speech patterns make it very difficult to phrase questions to get information. In Minnesota, I've heard people ask questions that beg a NO answer. For example: "Would you like to come to dinner, or no?" "Would you like to take this item home, or no?" "Can I help you, or no?" I suspect this anomaly has its roots in Northern European languages.

This may seem a small point, but I've found there is an unconscious conditioning powersports retailers seem to practice that solicits NO answers.

As I visit stores I count the number of "NO" signs displayed. Here's what I've found: A large sign directly behind the cash register that reads: "NO personal checks accepted." Another that reads, "NO returns without a receipt." Then there's, "NO refunds on electrical parts." The word NO is, most often, in large black letters; the rest of the sign in smaller red letters. The sign on the back of the cash register caps it all by saying, "NO credit card charges for purchases under $10.00."

In all these examples the word "NO" was the first and largest word on the signs. No wonder the customer is in a "NO" mood.

Why are we enforcing a negative response reaction by having signs that start with a big, bold - NO? I feel it's because the signs were made up by sign painters, not by people sensitive to marketing. NO creates an immediate defensive reaction. NO is hostile. YES feels better but can be an unnecessary gamble if the question asked has an either/or response.

It's interesting that the word NO in most languages also starts with the letter N, and they all sound harsh. In Russian the word for no, is niet; in German it's nine; in Scandinavian, nay. While in French, Spanish, Italian, Portuguese, and scores of other languages it's simply NO. The word yes, on the other hand, is oui; ya; da; aye or si, among hundreds of others.

Now for the other can't-do words. There are many negative attitude words to avoid when answering a customer's question. Negative attitude words include those which convey the idea that you're answering with a confirmed "NO."

Too often when the customer asks a salesperson a question the answer is preceded with: "Sorry we can't." Or. "I'd like to, but." Negative answers should be offered in a positive way. Avoid having your customer feel even the hint of disappointment before the deal is complete.

If you're asked to do something you know can't be done, instead of making a flat negative statement, buy time. You might suggest to the customer that you've never been asked that before and you'll have to check with management before you can answer. Although you know the response to a question may well be "NO," learn to let the customer down gently.

Don't spend too much time explaining why you can't do something, or why something doesn't work. The more you attempt to explain the more the customer will find contrary reasons. If you must tell someone the bad news be sure to follow up with some good news, even if it's light hearted.

Have I made my point, or no?

Chapter 28

PLAIN ENGLISH

When I began my career as a distributor's representative, I lived in Stone Mountain, Georgia. Visitors always wanted to see that great stone monument and the antebellum plantation at its base. I'd gladly take my guests there but soon grew tired of seeing the same old slave cabins. During one such visit, my friends had gone into the plantation while I went to the picnic area near the mountain's base. It was there I stumbled into an amateur radio swap meet.

One man was explaining to another that a particular piece of equipment would, "... work well on two meters and assure a good DX but," he went on, "you can expect a better reach if you use SSB." I had no earthly idea what they were talking about.

A few weeks later a friend related his frustration when he went into a camera store to buy what was to be his first good quality camera. He knew very little about cameras. The salesperson didn't help. He didn't ask what type of pictures my friend expected to take. He didn't determine how much my friend knew about cameras.

Instead the clerk (I won't call him a salesman. He was a clerk, which rhymes with jerk. Remember?) asked him if he wanted an SLR or an RF, and asked if he wanted 35, 110, 120 or a larger format? What "f" stop range did he need, and what ASA would he most often use? Obviously, this was prior to digital cameras becoming the norm. Now the questions are even more complex.

My friend left, feeling dumb, confused, angry and inadequate. The clerk (jerk) must have felt superior because he knew what the acronyms meant, but he didn't make a sale. My friend later bought a camera through a mail-order catalog because it was easier and he was able to learn about cameras by buying a couple of consumer photography magazines.

Are you guilty of talking in shorthand or a closed language? Do you use acronyms instead of talking in plain English?" Perhaps you don't think so, but I've discovered a large number of salespeople in the retail motorcycle business do speak in their own inside language. If you do, you stand a good chance of confusing an uninformed customer. A confused customer doesn't spend money. What do I consider closed language or shorthand speaking? References to: DOHC; 510x16; HD530x110; FX; GL, to name several.

Wouldn't it be easier to talk about the **Dual Overhead Cam** rather than telling an already confused customer the bike he wants has it? An HD530X110 is, as I'm sure you know, a heavy-duty chain with 110 links. But rather than asking the customer if that's what he needs, ask instead what he's riding. Once you know that you'll know what he needs and can be of greater help in guiding him.

Anyone in the camera business knows that an **SLR** refers to a **Single Lens Reflex** camera, and an **RF** refers to a **Range Finder** camera. A newcomer to the wonderful world of motorcycling may not know how big a cc is, or what the numbers on the side of the tires represent.

Why would anyone use acronyms and speak in a language not readily understood by the uninitiated? As we learn about an industry or hobby, part of that learning includes the special language associated with it. Some common words simply don't adequately describe the technology. To add to the dilemma, advertisers love to create new words and long descriptive phrases that lend themselves to acronyms. So, perhaps it's natural for us to speak in "shorthand."

Except for the military, the acronym language is most apparent in the world of computers. Anyone who has even a passing knowledge of computers knows what PC, XVGA, USB, RGB, CGA, RS232 and about two dozen other acronyms, mean. I wonder how many people were intimidated when they went to the computer store because they didn't understand what the salesperson was talking about.

Would more computers be in the hands of the general public if there was less confusion created by a new foreign language? I strongly feel there would be. The computer people talk about their PC computers as user-friendly. Their computer language isn't friendly at all.

Thank goodness for consumer magazines and Web sites. Their publishers find it helpful to define acronyms, even though most readers already know what they mean. We should follow their lead. We know that DOT stands for Department of Transportation and that CAFE stands for Corporate Average Fuel Economy. Everyone knows that MPG is the acronym for Miles Per Gallon, don't they? Then why do magazines use both the acronym and the entire name? The simple answer is, they do it for reasons of clarity and improved communications.

The importance of plain English to the print media is predicated on the fact they want their readers to read and understand the article. They don't know how well informed their readers are. Therefore, they make no assumptions. Instead they will communicate in such a way to minimize the chance for misunderstanding.

Newspapers, radio and television are very careful to avoid shorthand languages. Conventioneers and show exhibitors revel in using it. There is a certain satisfaction when speaking in shorthand languages. It allows those on the "inside" to differentiate themselves from "outsiders." It's an ego trip.

If you'd like to help the newcomer, consider printing a glossary of terms and acronyms that are most often used in your store and with your brands of bikes or accessories. Add some humor; it wouldn't hurt. When you hand your customer a manufacturer's brochure include your list of terms. Admit you have a special language. Spend the time defining shorthand terms as you use them in conversation with the customer, particularly if the customer is unfamiliar with the vernacular.

Those whose native language is not English, claim we have a very difficult language because there are so many definitions for each word. When combined with our use of slang and insider language, it's easy to understand why the problem is so frustrating.

Let's try to make things simpler, particularly when the customer is trying to buy something and needs guidance, not confusion. End the confusion or lose the customer.

Chapter 29

THE SILENT MARKET

Customers have changed more than retailers. The reason? Self-service has created the silent market. Self-service has also spawned the ever-growing mail-order and online business. If retailers in the powersports market want to grow they'll have to change the way they sell. I'm talking about a basic change; the change from a silent marketplace to a communicative one. The silent marketplace belongs to the mass merchandiser.

We must end the silent marketplace – that mute condition that prevents human contact and the exchange of ideas. Easily said, but it won't be easily accomplished.

For the past decade or more, we've been operating in this silent market. Let me give you some examples of how it works and why it's a problem we now face.

Major department stores, grocery stores, hardware stores and virtually every big box store have helped to create the silence. When you go grocery shopping, you don't have to say a word to anyone. You can push your cart up and down the isles and serve yourself.

If you need service, at the meat counter, for example, you'll have to ring the bell to get the butcher's attention. Few people go through the trouble. Big box stores have clerks standing by to take your money, but few know anything about the products they have for sale. So, it won't do much good to talk with them.

Many large stores spotlight individual products with demonstrations. They hire people to set up a small table and show the consumer the product. The stores expect this activity to increase sales of the demonstrated products to several hundred percent over self-service selections. It does because the silence is broken.

When you shop at the grocery store and you've made your selections, you enter the line at the checkout counter. When it's your turn to be served, you'll usually be asked questions that require a simple yes or no answer, or at best a one word response. "Will that be cash or check?" "Do you want plastic or paper bags?" The rest is inane monologue. "Thank you." Or my pet peeve: "Have a nice day."

If there was information you needed, you had to trust the labels on the goods, or you did your research before you went to the store. No one wants to talk to you, and I have a feeling, you don't want to talk to them either. The result? There is no exchange of ideas, no recommendations, and no one cares about you. Sad isn't it?

Because that's the way we've been treated, that's the way we treat other people – with silence. To overcome this condition some salespeople have resorted to talking continuously. They spout statistics, features and benefits, paint word pictures and do everything they can to inform and motivate the consumer. What too few of them do is get the customer to talk, to draw him out to find what he thinks, feels or wants.

The silent marketplace is allowed to function in order to protect the buyer and the seller from each other. A sad comment, but I believe it's true. As a result of this condition dealers feel they must carry every brand of every possible accessory, because the customer may want it. Few dealers carry what they truly believe in because they don't know how to talk to the consumer and persuade or guide him in making a purchase decision.

When a powersports dealer insists on having six brands of tires, five brands of helmets or four brands of motorcycles, it's usually because: "We get calls for it and don't want to lose sales." When that same dealer is asked by the customer which product is best, he's hard put to answer.

Experts are expected to have opinions. Most consumers expect the seller to be an expert as relates to the product, its features and benefits and competitive products. The customer expects to be asked questions and offered recommendations.

In short, retailers are supposed to know their products and tell consumers why they should buy it from them. This can't be done in the silent marketplace. Keep it silent and be prepared to emulate the chain grocery stores or big box retailers where the product simply becomes a commodity.

The entertainment industry has helped foster this silence. The Sylvester Stallone *Rambo* movies are, for all practical purposes, silent movies. Except for the bursts of explosives and gunfire. Stallone's lines could be written on the back of the matchbook. Clint Eastwood did the same thing in his early movies.

We began to believe that talking and listening were "out." Well folks... we've come full circle. If you don't want you customers to use mail-order, the interned, mass merchandisers or your competitor, break the silence. Ask him questions and listen to the answers.

Chapter 30

PSYCHOGRAPHICS

A New Way To Look At Buyers

Demographics, the statistical characteristics of populations, is, according to publications and manufacturers in the motorcycle industry a very important marketing tool. When they discuss demographics they mean the science that describes what people buy based on their age, education and income.

Most large manufacturers use demographics as a tool to position their product to appeal to specific segments of our population. Radio, TV, the Web and the printed form, all have packages of demographic profiles of their listeners, readers and users. These profiles are used to help advertisers interested in attracting customers who best fit the profile consistent with their marketing goals. If an advertiser is interested in selling computers, for example, he wouldn't advertise on an FM radio rock station. The demographics would tell him he'd get better results if he advertised on TV or on the Web.

While demographics is a valid marketing consideration, it has proven to be less than effective when applied to the recreational industry. The rules that apply to "needs" don't appear to be as effective when to apply to "wants." Today's more sophisticated customer has too many options and choices when he chooses to spend discretionary income on a leisure activity or hobby.

Psychographics is the study of why people buy what they do based on values and lifestyle. The term and idea were developed by the Science

Research Institute of California (where else?). While the research in this new science is still being developed, many large companies have already bought into the idea. Companies like Mercedes-Benz, Nissan, General Motors, Ford, Schlitz and Nike, to name a few, use psychographics as a marketing guide. They have paid millions of dollars to learn where they should spend tens of millions of dollars advertising their products and what their ads should say.

Why bother with psychographics? Because demographics can't explain why Jay Leno owns, loves and rides Harley-Davidsons. Nor can demographics explain why so many 45-year-old customers are buying their first motorcycle while the 25-year-old buyer is more interested in buying trucks and SUVs.

Everyone in a marketing capacity in our industry knows that demographics have failed us. Motorcycles are supposed to appeal to one particular set of buyers based on demographics, but instead the sport appeals to an entirely different group or groups.

We talk about the graying of America. What about the graying of the American motorcyclist? It used to be a young man's sport. Now the average age of a motorcyclist is approaching 40; far from the 18- to 25-year-old category we targeted in the past based on demographics.

In order to tap into the psyche of who's likely to buy motorcycles and other powersports units, it will be necessary to identify subgroups of buyers based on their values and life styles.

What follows are **categories** I've identified and labeled to aid in recognizing who the players are and how you'll have to deal with them.

Because we're all more or less familiar with demographics, I've taken the liberty of including some demographics criteria within the psychographics profiles. What that means is the results may be suspect and subjective.

Psychographic Categories

THE DEDICATED cover a wide age group; from 20 to over 60. These are the rally folks. Although some may be young most are older. Even the younger members of this group appear older than their years. They are not explorers. They like to go to the same place every year. They are non-smokers and very light or non-drinkers. They don't like to try new food, places or things. The dedicated insist on the familiar. They have trouble communicating with people outside their group, although they are fair talkers and ask a lot of questions.

> **How to Sell to the Dedicated:** This segment is interested only in proven products. The motorcycle must be a tried-and-proved model. Apparel, helmets and accessories should be well advertised and well accepted products.
>
> Show them the newer products only if they seem interested. If they don't, it will only confuse them.
>
> Use referrals from other members of the group. Take care not to exaggerate the benefits or misstate features. Take it slow and easy. Gain their confidence.

THE GADGET HOUND has a narrower age span; about 35 to 55 years of age. They have a high feeling of self worth. They have a tendency to be better educated and very "high-tech" oriented. They are interested in anything "new," but don't relate well to people.

This is the subgroup that will buy a first year unproven product. They are pleasant guys but often distant. They have many hobbies and interests. Many are wrench twisters. They like to go to new places, try new foods, listen to a wide range of music but they're very cost conscious.

The Gadget Hound is the largest buyer group in the powersports world. On the negative side, this group complains the most, and is the least understanding of things not perfect. The Gadget Hound has a good vocabulary and enjoys using it. He loves talking motorcyclese.

How to Sell to the Gadget Hound: Show this customer the latest, trickest thing you have. Use statistics and carefully describe features and benefits.

Let the customer know you're aware he is interested in "leading edge" products. Take care that you don't get too personal.

JOINERS may be from 30 to 45. This group has only a fair feeling of self worth. They feel threatened by things they don't understand. They like the company of others with similar interests. They "join the club" because that's what's important to them. They're strong believers in God and country. They're very conservative and most live monotonous lives.

The joiners ride short distances. They are easily scared away by safety considerations. They're very family oriented people and are into church-going and golf. Exploring is not a high priority for this group but saving money for a rainy day, is. As for communication skills, this group listens intently but says little.

How to Sell to Joiners: Take your time. Carefully explain everything while you watch their reactions. If they appear puzzled, go back and make sure they understand before you continue. Watch your language. If you use profanity you may lose the sale.

Demonstrators and last year's models are good choices because of the savings. Even if it's old it must be well kept and have a good appearance.

VACATIONERS are in the 25 to 50 age group. They're not physically active. This group is more likely to be smokers and drinkers. They believe in play and work. They are trend followers, not trendsetters. They're very brand conscious and will follow a strong leader although they're very suspicious of authority. Vacationers are great talkers but can easily become boring.

How to Sell to Vacationers: Take them to the best advertised products. Show them what's "In." Take care to avoid technical explanations. Stress the acceptance of the products and relate to how "everyone likes this one."

SEEKERS consist of the 25 to 45 age group. They're conservative achievers with high goals. They set aside specific time for leisure activities. The seeker is gregarious and outgoing. He travels with a wallet full of credit cards. They like others to believe they know more than they do. Seekers speak well but are impatient. However, they are inclined to be less critical of others.

How to Sell to Seekers: Seekers appear to want to know all the specifications but as soon as you start telling them they change the subject. Be patient, let them talk and don't interrupt. If they like it, they'll buy it. The price isn't as important to them as owning something they are going to use. Tell them of activities in which they may want to participate.

UPPERS are aggressive 20- to 35-year-old subgroup. They are urban, money-hungry compulsives. They follow fashions and trends. Designer labels are very important to this group. They like the one-off idea and feel whatever they have should be different. The Uppers are very competitive. Uppers speak faster than most other subgroups, although their choice of words often misses the mark. When they ask questions they want an instant reply.

How to Sell to Uppers: This group responds well to custom bikes and to high performance, high visibility motorcycles. They may claim that price is no object but they have clearly defined financial limits. Determine how much they are willing to spend before you get in too deeply involved in selling a particular unit.

WANDERERS are an older group and consist of those aged 40 and up. They respond to the "call of the wild." Wanderers are campers and value human relationships. They live in the saddle. They're interested in the ecology of our planet, not in technical gimmicks.

The Wanderers take up lost causes. They have strong opinions and are often argumentative. Wanderers speak very well and have large vocabularies. They love to exchange ideas with others who share their views about the world. However, they don't like to talk motorcyclese.

> **How to Sell to Wanderers:** Their interests lie in good used and reliable bikes. If some of the luxury features are missing, that's OK with them. If they appear to want to challenge you, let them win. Winning is very important to this group; they're sore losers.

WANABEES are the young ones; they're 17 to 25 years old. This is a hard-working group. They want better than they can afford. Because they are young they have a tendency to be more idealistic and are often dreamers. Wanabees have unrealistic goals yet strong opinions. They're difficult to inform or educate but believe the printed word and trusted Web sources are gospel. This group has poorly developed communications skills. Their limited vocabularies are offset by their gestures and pauses for validation. This is the group that uses "like" and "ya-know" liberally sprinkled in their sentences.

> **How to Sell to Wanabees:** Wanabees should be carefully directed away from state-of-the-art high-tech, high priced units, although that's what they come in to buy. Why? They can't afford it and won't buy anything if they decide that what they are going to have to settle for is "second best." Carefully explain to them the advantages of less expensive, smaller, easier to handle bikes. Let them read the test reports and any other literature to support your sales pitch.

Like most others who have been exposed to the Psychographics concept, as you read the traits of each subgroup you probably identified people you know who match one or more of the traits described. There may be some of your friends, associates or customers who appear to have split personalities at least as it relates to psychographics. That is, they appear to have characteristics that fit two or more headings.

Psychographics is not an exact science. It will, however, give you a different perspective when viewing customers. How you relate to them, once you've identified their tendencies, may mean the difference between filling their needs and satisfying their wants, or having them go elsewhere.

Chapter 31

YOUR WEB SITE

The Web is essential today. Does yours make the grade? Are you making customers aware of it?

And is there an advantage to reducing your Yellow Pages ads in favor of a dynamic Web site? In a word, yes.

Today, unlike in the past, people use the Yellow Pages to simply look up a phone number. I suggest that if you accept this reality you reduce the size of your phone book ad. It should now contain nothing more than your hours, directions, phone number, perhaps brand names you sell and the largest possible font with your web site's URL.

Although the Web has been with us for more than a decade it has now passed the critical mass mode and has become THE de-facto communications tool.

According to the latest Pew Internet study available as of this writing in December 2004, nearly 60 percent of American adults go online. That translates into 120,000,000 people. The percentage rises among younger people. Between 69 and 72 percent of those under the age of 50 go online.

The numbers are even higher for the better-educated, higher-income consumer. A full 80 percent of those who make over $50,000 a year go online. Among the college educated, 82 percent go online.

What do all these online surfers do? They (1) use email, (2) search for information and (3) buy products.

Consider also that the average shift in population of any city is reported by the census bureau to be approximately 17 percent. What that means is that during a three-year period half the people that live in your town moved there within the recent past. How do these new residents find you?

No, not by using the Yellow Pages; they go on the Web and do a search.

The Internet is a marketing paradigm. The Christmas season of 2004 saw Internet retail sales grow four times faster than brick and mortar stores. Purchasers feel comfortable using their credit cards to make their buys. Even banks now indemnify users who make their purchases in cyberspace.

So, what does all this mean? It means that you MUST have a Web site. **The site must be dramatic, dynamic and updated at least weekly.**

What is the benefit of a quality site? You have the ability to expand your market from a local one to, as the name implies, a World Wide Web. And even in your local market you can attract more visitors to your store if they can first find you and check you out on the Web.

Unless you are tremendously adept at Web design, you need to hire professionals to design and build your site. Your Web site needs to look professional and make a good first impression. You don't necessarily have to spend a great deal of money on the design. Just make sure the end result looks as professional as you want your store to look. After all, your Web site may be the first thing a new customer sees, even before your store.

Every local community has fine Web designers. Some Web designers even specialize by industry. For example, there are designers who focus on the powersports industry. So you should have plenty to choose from.

Web design is a very involved and highly technical process. I can't cover all the factors that need to be taken into account. That said, however, I can give you basic guidelines for what a good powersports Web site needs to include.

What To Include On Your Site

At a minimum, your Web site should include these elements:

Home page

Make this page into a workhorse for you! It should be attractive and updated regularly. Include your dealership name and logo, your hours of operation, address and telephone number, and a link to an interactive map through Mapquest or Yahoo maps. After all, most users will be looking for this information.

Remember, a picture is worth 1,000 words. Grab the customer's attention with a few attractive pictures of the units and accessories you carry. A good close-up of the interior showroom can serve this purpose. Some dealers also include the brand names they sell and the logos. Don't waste this valuable home page "real estate" with a huge photo of the exterior of your dealership!

Consider adding a box for a weekly special. The box will need to be updated regularly. This keeps the site dynamic and interesting, and gives customers a reason to come back.

If you offer a newsletter, an email signup box is a must. Dealers with eCommerce initiatives should also include prominent "above the scroll" links to drive users into their online store.

About

Humans are naturally curious. Studies have shown that the "About" section is one of the most highly clicked in most Web sites. This section should personalize your dealership. Show pictures of happy smiling customers! They'll love it and so will new prospects. Include pictures of key staff, including the dealer principal and the general manager. Be sure to include names, titles and a way to contact each one through email and/or phone. And, yes, the "About" section is where the picture of your dealership building belongs. Make it as big as you want in this section.

Units

Make the effort to colorfully describe the lines you carry with attractive photographs. Motorcyclists and powersports enthusiasts love to look at pictures of the things they want. You'll find they do most of their Web surfing at work and in the winter, when they can't be out riding. Show them enough, along with descriptive text, to make them want to visit your store.

Service and Parts

Use these two sections to describe the service department and parts department hours, any specials, and prominent contact information including email, phone and address. Even though you may have this information on the home page, don't make the user hunt for it. The best Web sites have deliberate redundancy.

Events and Clubs

If you sponsor a club or rally, then it should have a dedicated page on your site. Load digital photos of the last ride or other fun event, and you'll have visitors flocking to your site again and again. Better yet, allow visitors to post comments about the event.

Your Specialty

Add other product sections for the products you sell the most. If you sell large numbers of used bikes, for instance, consider a dedicated section for used bikes. Just remember that if you add it, you have to update it. Nothing is worse than an obviously outdated page. And you certainly don't want to deal with the prospective customer who calls all excited about that used bike he saw on your site, only to learn it was sold six months ago.

Navigation Links

Every page should have clearly labeled navigation links or buttons. More is **not** better. Studies have shown that five to seven top-level navigation links are the optimum number, and won't confuse visitors with too many choices.

Give enticing but descriptive names to navigation links. "Vehicle Showroom" or "Bikes" will get more clicks than a dry word like "Products."

Online Store

Selling online now is like having a completely separate retail business. I know of one dealer who actually sells more than a million dollars of goods, mostly parts and apparel, per month. He has a 500-or-more page site and professionals keeping it updated.

Make the decision to sell online, thoughtfully. Do you have the ability to promptly fulfill online orders? What about returns? Do you have sufficient staff to respond to customer service emails? What about updating product descriptions, adjusting prices, running specials?

If you have made the plunge to sell online – eCommerce – then you are probably well ahead of this Chapter. Just be sure that you have prominent "above the scroll" links to your online store throughout your site.

Privacy Policy

Every Web site should have a privacy policy if you are collecting information from visitors, such as email addresses or credit card information. There are plenty of sample policies on the Web. Certain browsing security settings can block sites without privacy policies.

Copyright Notice

This should be at the bottom of each page in small font. Make sure it is updated to reflect the current year. Outdated copyright dates exude an air of cobwebs and disuse.

Under Construction Pages

No! No! No! Under no circumstances should you ever have a page on your site labeled "under construction." If it's not finished, then take down all links leading to that page until you can get it finished.

Technology Choices

One of the great things about technology is that it is constantly evolving and improving. Web site owners today have a myriad of choices of technology to build sites. And the good news is that the price keeps dropping. Never before has it cost less to set up a basic Web site. I expect technology prices to continue to fall, as technology becomes a commodity.

I won't try to tell you which technology to use. Most likely my advice would be outdated by the time you are reading this book anyway. I can tell you a few things to avoid: annoying series of pop-ups (the quickest way to turn off your site visitors), Flash software (search engines find it tough to index sites in Flash and some browsers don't recognize it), frames (search engines, again), text on black backgrounds (too hard to read), or hidden or invisible text designed to fool search engines (it doesn't and may get your site banned).

Hosting

Outsource your site hosting to a professional service. Don't try to host your site on your premises. The cost of hosting today is so low that it is not worth the hassle to do it internally. Professional hosting costs a fraction of what it would have cost a few years ago. Hosting has also improved dramatically, getting more reliable. Most hosting services deliver 99 percent or better uptime – even though you'll never get them to guarantee it!

Besides, any good hosting company can provide you with all manner of visitor statistics and tracking reports to understand how many people visit your site, how they get there and what they look at. Often this service is provided at no additional cost to you. They also are better equipped to take care of security issues in this day of hacking attacks, viruses, etc.

GETTING PEOPLE TO YOUR SITE

Unfortunately, putting up a site is just the beginning. Getting the search engines to find you and give you a high listing takes work. You can hire professionals for this task. It's called search engine optimization (SEO). These professionals will adjust your site so that all the content is easily read anytime a search engine "bot" drops by for a crawl. That way your site has a better chance of getting a high listing.

There are other things you can do, too:

1) Make sure your site is listed in powersports industry directories and OEM dealer directories. Make sure it's not just a text listing. You want a hyperlink back to your home page. The same goes for general directories like Yahoo and DMOZ. Many of these listings are free.

2) Purchase online advertising. The most cost effective advertising is something called pay-per-click advertising. Pay-per-click means that you pay only when someone clicks through and visits your site – and stays for at least 30 to 90 seconds. The two 900 pound gorillas of pay-per-click advertising – and the only ones that really count – are Google AdWords and Overture.

3) Make sure your Web address is listed on every piece of paper in your dealership: business cards, letterhead, invoices, brochures.

4) Assign responsibility for updating your site and attracting visitors to one of your staff. This duty has to be treated as seriously as any other the employee has, not an afterthought or a "nice to do." **Remember: inspect what you expect.** If you ask about it and your staff knows you are interested in the Web site, it will get more attention. And you'll get better results from it.

Chapter 32

THE CHANGING CONSUMER

The Aging Rider

For reasons I don't understand it appears that each generation is labeled. It makes no sense to me to label an entire generation, but we do it anyway. Keeping track of the labels is like keeping track of the terrorist threat index colors. I'm not sure if those in their mid-20s are "Gen-X" or some other cryptic code but I can tell you that the sampling to give such a title to millions can't be supported by empirical data.

Those who report on demographics tell us that America is "graying." Those of us in the powersports industry have seen the aging process close up and personal. Attend any rally and you'll see more bald and gray heads than full hair heads. More mature riders are riding big touring bikes and are less interested in being the first one away from the stoplight. Being able to lean over until sparks fly does not impress these riders, either. They are more likely to follow the "stop and smell the roses" philosophy of riding.

For the past several decades the average motorcyclist age was going up and doing so at an alarming rate. Way back, when I was on the Board of Directors of the American Motorcyclist Association (AMA), the average age of a motorcyclist was 24. Today it's well over 40.

Does this mean today's riders are the last segment and there is little hope for continued growth in the motorcycle industry? No, it means the opposite.

Let's take a look at the graying rider. According to the research done by the AMA, the Motorcycle Industry Council (MIC) and many of the OEMs, today's aged riders have high incomes, are well educated and married.

They also have children. That's where the next crop of riders will come from.

The Aging Rider's Children

Many of those "retreads" and those approaching the terrifying status of senior citizen rider have sons and daughters in their 20s and even (gulp) 30s. These "kids" if one can call a 25-year-old a kid, are the perfect prospect for becoming enthusiastic motorcycle owners. It's unlike generations ago when it was a struggle to convince your parents that motorcycles were not bad and that if they just would let you ride one you wouldn't speed or use booze. You would promise to wear protective clothing and a helmet. Even then it was a pretty hard sell.

The energy crises of the '70s and early '80s gave us ammunition by enabling us to talk about the advantages of riding a motorcycle because back then they got much better mileage than the average "cage." We gave those rationalizations to our parents and, if we'd made the plunge into marriage, our spouses.

The necessity to convince today's motorcycle owning, motorcycle riding, enthusiastic Mom or Dad is an easy sell. They know the added value motorcycles have given their lifestyles. They don't have to be persuaded of the positive attributes motorcycles represent. They know too that their peers consider them risk takers and non-conformists. They know too that those same peers secretly and often overtly, envy them.

This 17- to 30-year-old son or daughter of a "with it" motorcycle parent won't necessarily buy the same type of bike Mom or Dad rides. That wouldn't be cool. They grew up knowing that their parents were different. They believed it was a freedom of choice thing. They grew up around motorcycles. They rode on the back of Mom or Dad's bike. They couldn't wait until they grew up and got their first motorcycle license.

The best part is they're coming to a store near you; perhaps to your store. So, be ready to deal with the new/old customer. They may be new to you but not new when it comes to buying into the lifestyle.

Do these children of motorcycling parents need to be treated differently? The simple answer is, yes. Many of them may know more about motorcycles than the person attempting to sell them. They will probably know more about the history and development of bikes than the average customer. Chances are they'll want to talk about their experiences growing up in a motorcycle owning family. Your best option: listen.

You may discover that brand loyalty is less important to them than your ability and willingness to work with them. As most of you know, the people in this age group are more than a bit skeptical when dealing with salespeople. They often come in with "defense" written in invisible letters across their foreheads.

It's going to be up to you to win them over. That means you can't fake it. Many of them have a life-long motorcycle background although this might be their first purchase of a bike.

Is there a way to prevent sales gaffes? I think there is. That way is to ask questions and listen carefully to the answers. Canned sales pitches won't work with these savvy prospects. You can probably handle it without too much angst. However, when the prospect is a woman, take extra care. Historically, women weren't as knowledgeable as most men when it came to motorcycles. <u>**These**</u> women, however, were brought up surrounded by motorcycles.

If you get into the habit of asking questions before you make statements or suggestions you stand less risk of alienating this group of buyers. You also stand less of a chance of embarrassing yourself. Let me modify that. If you get into the habit of asking questions of any prospective buyer you'll increase your chance of making a sale, period.

WOMEN RIDERS

Data being reported in the industry suggests that recently the overall age of motorcyclists mysteriously started going **down**, despite the obvious graying of the Baby Boomer population. This anomaly seemed difficult to explain, given aging Baby Boomer demographics.

It was, until I talked to an old friend who also happens to be a multi-line dealer in Knoxville, Tennessee, Dile Brown. Dile doesn't look at things the way most people do and he certainly doesn't just go along with "conventional wisdom."

As we discussed the age anomaly Dile suggested that perhaps there was one factor that was not considered in the reports: the gender factor. No, I had never considered it. Sure, I knew that more bikes were being sold to women and more OEMs were offering motorcycles with lower seat height to accommodate women who on average are several inches shorter than men. But I never put the proverbial two and two together.

Let's take a look at the gender factor and see what it does to alter that conventional wisdom. Suppose, for example that brand XX is primarily a heavyweight motorcycle and the average age of the male rider is, say 50. Enter the gender factor. About 10 years ago the percentage of women motorcycle owners was almost negligible; perhaps only two or three percent. Now, according to those same researchers, the percentage has gone double-digit.

Few "older" (hang on while I step on the edge of the politically correct paradigm) women, those over 30, opt to become motorcyclists having never been so inclined before. On the other hand many 40- and 50-something men are new or re-entry riders.

Let's say that brand XX has been selling 100,000 motorcycles per year and 97 percent of the buyers are men with an average age of 50. The other 3 percent are women with an average age of 30. That brings the overall average of brand XX motorcycle riders to 49.4 years of age.

Let's increase the percentage of women from three to today's percentage of about 10. Now the overall average age drops to 45.3 assuming that I've done the math right. So, brand XX OEM now reports that they don't have to worry about the ageing motorcyclist because the average age of their riders has mysteriously dropped by four years.

So, where's the truth about the aging motorcycling population? Until researchers go out and do a head count we'll never know for certain.

However, I think it's safe to assume that the average age of male motorcyclists is actually continuing to climb – as a group they're getting older. One reason is the cost of units. Touring bikes, cruisers and large displacement performance bikes, which account for a very large percentage of units sold, now sell for well over $15,000.

The women's market, however, as a whole, is younger.

In reality, we now have two markets besides those relating to niche products. One is the male market, the other female. Harley-Davidson has addressed this issue by creating more women's styles of clothing and has made an attempt to create bikes that appeal to the feminine market albeit with limited success.

The importers have attempted to address similar issues with even less success. The MIC and AMA have both attempted to address the elusive feminine market. Don't get me wrong, the OEMs and industry associations have had some success considering that the percentage of women riders has tripled in the past decade. A quick look at the Internet reveals there are more than 50 sites dedicated to women motorcyclists. There are consumer print magazines created to address women motorcyclists. It's obvious that they are having an impact or we couldn't see so many women riders as we do today.

I think it's important for dealers to look for new ways to attract younger riders as well as finding ways to get more women involved in the sport. However, these are two distinctly separate tasks requiring creative thinking and planning.

As I travel and visit dealerships I now see more women salespeople on the floor. No, the women are not exclusively relegated to the parts or apparel sales; many are on the floor selling motorcycles. I've also discovered that these women seem to know more about the features and benefits of the motorcycles and seem to have a better grasp of the selling process than their male counterparts.

Obviously, women are better at selling to other women than are men. All too often a male salesperson will act in a condescending manner when selling to a woman. Nothing infuriates women more than being the recipient of information meted out by a man who seems to feel he has to talk slowly and carefully so she can understand him.

What can we expect in the future? I expect to see the focus of motorcycling shift to smaller displacement, lighter bikes and more activities that involve women and entire families. Only time will tell, but I sure hope I'm right.

Chapter 33

YOUR DMS

Recent years have been very positive as a whole for the powersports industry, despite the volatile economy, currency fluctuations and war drums. Most dealers seem to have prospered in recent years. Unit sales continue to rise. ATVs continue to outsell motorcycles. The reliability of motorcycles, watercraft, snowmobiles and ATVs continues to improve. Replacement parts have fewer back orders. So it would seem there's nothing to complain about, right? Wrong!

As I visit and phone dealers to discuss what's happening in their markets few have anything negative to say except that they are having a hard time finding qualified employees. When they talk about their DMS systems, however, they become animated and begin to list their grievances.

Obviously, all franchised dealers now have some sort of DMS or dealer management system. OK, so let's call it what it really is: a computer system that allows you to run your business more efficiently.

In the early days of computers in powersports retail stores the programs were either off-the-shelf or custom written. Back then bank reconciliation, special order notification, departmental profitability, and individual employee efficiency were not things which concerned dealers. Back then there were few dealers with gross sales of over $10 million dollars.

Today there are more than a dozen DMS providers who supply software to the powersports industry. Of them, a few dominate the market with a combined market share of well over 70 percent. These few major providers have been in business for more than a decade and have constantly upgraded and updated their systems. Most have moved from proprietary platforms to Windows ™.

Years ago, few dealers needed more than, say, 20 workstations. Today, it's not uncommon for multi-line dealers and those who sell more than $50 million per year to have many more workstations. Still others have multi-locations with well over 75 terminals.

These are sophisticated dealers indeed. So why are they complaining about their systems?

It didn't take me long to discover the source of the problem. No, it isn't related to "bugs" in the software. No, it's not related to hardware issues. And, no, it's not a problem with the complexity of the software. So what is the problem? It appears to be the skills of the staff responsible for getting information into and out of the system.

Today, almost every dealer is vitally interested in detailed reports to show how things are going compared to the previous day, month or year. Today, a dealer wants to be sure not to accept a check from a customer who had given him an NSF check in the past. Special "deals," incentives, promotions, gift certificates, discounts, spiffs, commissions, etc., are all part of everyday business. However, they create real customer satisfaction problems if they are not carefully documented and addressed.

Your system, more than likely, has the ability to tell you who gets a regular discount, who should pay cash only, who owes you money and who is a general pain in the backside. That information should pop up as soon as you identify the customer. If it doesn't, you'd best contact your DMS provider and find out how to do it.

Here's what's real: about one in 10 dealers uses **all** the DMS modules and has the ability to create all the reports he needs to stay on top of what's happening. The other nine have problems created by new employees who have not been trained or procedures that have not been documented and made a part of the employee's operational responsibilities.

DMS Training

The larger DMS providers have a dedicated staff of support people. In addition to being technically adept, some are specialists in accounting, invoicing, inventory control, report generating, etc. They also offer on-site or home office training. The training is specialized and in some cases, involves multi-day sessions. However, many of the DMS providers report that they find it difficult to convince their users to come in to get trained.

Are there training options? Sure are. Several provide regional training. A few have self-pacing training via the Internet. At least two offer training in your store. The latter option has pluses and minuses. On the plus side you'll be using your equipment in your store with all your staff. On the minus side: cost, interruptions and distractions.

Considering that the powersports industry has a turnover of about 30 percent per year it should be obvious that there's a desperate need to bring new people on board and, more importantly, see that they receive the necessary training.

While visiting dealers recently I interviewed department managers. Those in charge of accounting often complained that their system didn't do many of the tasks they needed. When I asked about their training most told me of their formal education to become bookkeepers or accountants. When I asked about their formal training on the use of the computer-based accounting programs, the common response was: "What training?" The same was true of the parts managers, sales managers and yes, even the dealer principal.

I then asked about a line item in their budgets for training, specifically formal computer-related training. Much to my surprise only a very few had such a line item. The rest believed that the systems should be more intuitive and understand what they wanted without having to be specific in their requests. Well folks, this ain't Star Trek or Andromeda. Computers don't talk to us and then use extrapolated logic to determine what we really meant. In short, YOU NEED MORE TRAINING!

Most of the problems I've alluded to in this Chapter are there because of the lack of training. With the high turnover of personnel at vital points like the checkout kiosk, the apparel department and the parts counter, the highest priority must be training. After all, there's where the money is.

Following are six items I believe are important if you expect to continue to grow and prosper.

LEVERAGING YOUR DMS FOR CONTINUED GROWTH

1. Set up a line item in your budget for DMS training
2. Contact your DMS provider and get the training schedule
3. Schedule **every** department for training
4. If you're the dealer principal make sure you include yourself in training
5. Demand accountability after training
   - When the staff member returns from training have him report to you and outline what he has learned
6. Be specific in your expectations
   - You should expect better reporting and greater efficiencies from all departments once they are trained

A sage once said: "If you think education is expensive, try ignorance." I'm not a sage; however, I've been in this business long enough to know that we must all continue to learn but that in order to we need qualified teachers. Finally, as one dealer succinctly put it: "If you don't train, you really can't complain."

DMS HARDWARE

You are going to have to accept the distasteful fact that computer programs must be updated constantly to meet the ever-changing OEM, governmental and accounting requirements. You are also going to have to understand that your staff will need to be trained to learn how to accomplish some of these complex and daunting tasks.

Next, you'll need to accept the reality that the useful life of your computer hardware is about three years.

No, that doesn't mean you're going to have to replace the screens and printers every three years. It just means it may be an advantage to do so. For example, are you still using the big box CRT monitors? LCD monitors have come down in price and take up considerably less space.

New high quality, super fast printers, which used to cost thousands, can now be purchased for a few hundred dollars – or less. High-resolution color printers capable of reproducing photo quality graphics have seen dramatic price drops. However, many have switched from using parallel printer connections to USB1 or the latest USB2 or Firewire. Do your current computers have Firewire or USB ports to connect these new efficient printers?

Many of the new backup systems now rely on CDR or CDRW or DVD-R or DVD-RW instead of older tape backups. This doesn't even factor in the newer Dual Layer DVD. These new systems require different drivers, however, and that means your DMS provider has even more upgrades to consider. By the time you read this book there will be some other new technology improvement that hasn't been envisioned yet.

Don't get me wrong, I'm not advocating you go out and buy the latest and greatest hardware. Why? Because it probably will be less reliable than what you have now. Besides, buying the latest will mean you'll need even more training. But there can be real advantages to upgrading.

Remember: If you know **how** to use your DMS properly, taking the time to learn its features and make sure your employees are using them, your system can have a major positive impact on your store's profitability.

P.S. If the acronyms used in this Chapter have you scratching your head, the following list tells you what they mean.

ACRONYM LIST

CD-R = Write once Compact Disk 650mb or 700mb capacity.

CD-RW = Write, re-write many times Compact Disk 650mg or 700mb capacity.

DMS = Dealer Management System: computer hardware and software.

DVD-R = Digital Video Disc write once 4.7gb capacity. Records video or data.

DVD-RW = Digital Video Disc re-write many times. 4.7gb capacity.

Firewire = External connection faster than USB1 about equal to USB2. Commonly used for video also for remote hard drive.

USB1 = Universal Serial Bus. 1st iteration.

USB2 = Universal Serial Bus. Second iteration; much faster, backwards compatible.

Dual Layer DVD = Hardware and software are becoming available to support the new dual layer protocol. These can store almost 10gb of data. Wait until the media prices drop before upgrading to this new storage method. In the meantime, you can purchase a 120gb USB or Firewire hard drive to back up data for less than $200.00.

Chapter 34

SERVICE DEPARTMENTS

For many years powersports service departments were considered necessary evils. Few were profitable. Most drained cash from the dealership. Owners complained that service departments were costly to staff. They cited the need to buy special and sometimes very expensive shop tools and seldom realized a return on their investment. Now, thankfully, that's changing.

What brought about the change? Three things:

(1) the insistence of the OEMs,

(2) the desire of dealerships to minimize customer angst, and

(3) the emergence of the quest for improving CSI (Customer Satisfaction Index) scores.

Add to that dealers' ability to order parts online, their comprehensive computer systems, and management who are now keenly aware of the costs and efficiencies of operating profitable service departments.

The training of staff has and continues to be a critical factor. Obviously, the technicians need to be schooled in the procedures of servicing specific models. They need to know the specifications and have the tools necessary to conduct service efficiently.

The dealership needs to have the appropriate special tools and equipment for the techs to use. Management must know what it takes to operate such a labor-intensive department profitably. But where does the information come from? The OEM provides a large segment of it but there is still much to learn in order to become and remain truly profitable.

Some types of motorcycles require considerably more service than others. Off-road bikes and ATVs are used in very harsh circumstances where falling down, crashing and breaking things are common. High performance bikes trade off reliability for the sake of performance. Riders who "flog" their machines require more service than those who have greater respect for their steeds. Some bikes are platforms for customizing and modifying.

Service departments have needs that differ from other departments in the store. However, they must rely on and work closely with the parts department. Without that cooperation service can come to a standstill.

Today, few dealerships have all the special tools they need and often must rely on outside sources to do some of the very special work. Plating, painting, milling, machining, frame straightening, etc. are often done by outside firms. That means a service department staff member must be capable of assessing the skill level of the vendors and spend time visiting with them to maintain a mutually beneficial relationship.

It takes years of experience and training to create a profitable, efficient service department.

All OEMs use some sort of CSI to evaluate their dealers. No dealership can ever achieve a high CSI unless it has an efficient and well-run service department. If I were to list the five major departments in order of their importance in CSI scoring and the ability to create customer loyalty they would be as follows:

1. Service
2. Sales
3. Parts
4. Accessories
5. F&I

Here's what's real. If your customer never has a problem you might get a very high CSI and develop a relatively loyal customer. If the customer does have a problem and you solve it quickly, to his or her satisfaction, you'll have a very loyal customer who will influence his or her friends to use your services.

Where are the problems likely to show up? When the customer comes in for service – either warranty or any other service. Every department makes promises. Some are kept and, unfortunately, some are not. Most customers seem to be able to forgive sales, parts, accessory and F&I departments for infractions. Few are willing to forgive the service department for anything but very minor flubs.

A service department is like a hospital. When you or a family member needs attention at a hospital few are very forgiving of errors, hence, the steep malpractice insurance premiums paid by doctors and hospitals. We are fortunate that few service departments are required to have such special insurance policies.

Honestly evaluate your service department. If it is in need of an overhaul – whether to achieve higher CSI ratings for the OEMs or to improve your bottom line – consider getting specialized help. Bring in one of the industry's few, rare, service department professionals.

The goal? Efficiency, profitability and higher CSI.

Chapter 35

DEALERSHIP CONSOLIDATION

Despite the stock market disintegration of the early 21st century, terrorism scares, dollar uncertainty and a recession, the motorcycle industry continues to grow at double-digit percentages. It's as if our industry has absolutely nothing do to with the rest of the country's economy or mood. Meanwhile the consolidators continue to look for more viable acquisitions, mergers and consolidation opportunities.

The first rumors about consolidation at the dealership level surfaced in the late 1990s. Since then a lot has happened. Now, it seems that a great deal more is about to happen despite the general economic situation in the USA. There are both rumors and real action of consolidation of motorcycle publications, dealerships, warehouse distributors and even manufacturers.

When consolidation first came to the attention of the industry, many said it wouldn't work. Obviously, it is working at least on some levels. One example is the consolidation or at least very aggressive joint activities of Suzuki and Kawasaki. There has also been consolidation of some of Europe's motorcycle OEMs.

When talking about dealer consolidation most suggested the jury is still out. Their reasoning seemed logical. This is an enthusiasts' industry, they say. What will happen when the "suits" are calling the shots? Will it be us versus them? Would they soon tire of the meager profits and long hours we've become accustomed to? Would the OEMs agree to have one company own so many dealerships with competing brands? What would happen if the economy continues to weaken? Will these "suits" simply shut down and go away? These and more questions began to circulate. However, predicting what might happen based on economic theories is an exercise in futility. Industry-wide consolidation is the wave that is changing our marketplace.

At first dealer consolidation created considerable angst among some of the OEMs. One simply terminated their relationship – canceling the agreement, repurchasing the inventory – with the dealership rather than allow this outside company to purchase it. Another was involved in litigation when a group of dealers wanted to consolidate. Who won? The lawyers.

One OEM was rather pragmatic, feeling there was no downside to consolidation as long as the consolidator had the funds, the people and the desire to make it work.

Consolidation was the hot topic of conversation at trade events. Everyone wanted to see what would happen while most predicted it wouldn't work long-term. As the general economy began its nosedive in the early 2000s, the naysayers felt vindicated believing our industry would soon show signs of growing weakness. As of this writing in late 2004, it hasn't weakened. In fact we continue to grow at double-digit percentages, thereby confounding all the prognosticators, me included.

One consolidator hit the ground running and soon ran into problems. Apparently he didn't understand the relationship between the dealer and the OEM. Another, America's PowerSports, Inc., took it slow, painfully slow, I thought. Their acquisition model seemed cast in stone. That model was to look for stores doing at least $8 million in sales with solid profits, excellent reputation in the community and with their OEMs and strong management willing to stay on board.

They are one of the most aggressive and successful dealer consolidators in the powersports industry. Their track record speaks for itself: dozens of franchises (all major OEMs represented, including Harley). They own multiple dealerships in several states. Their sales exceed $100 million. They employ hundreds of well-paid staff and show profits that would be the envy of most dealerships.

What does consolidation mean for the industry and what lessons can be learned?

For one thing, it means greater operational efficiency.

Recently I received some interesting statistics from Lightspeed, the ADP DMS provider, about running dealerships based on efficiency.

If you employ 2.2 or 2.0 people per million dollars in sales, consider yourself very efficient. If the store did $10 million in sales per year, a staff of 20 to 22 would be very efficient. Each additional employee over that number represents a substantial bottom line dollar difference.

If you fall into the 2.0 to 2.2 employees per million, you use your computer as a tool to keep you abreast of what's happening and you have reports that are up to the minute. You have the ability to use the numbers to help guide your business.

You are also a good manager and are **working on, rather than in**, the business. Chances are you belong to at least one 20 club and have a good knowledge of accounting or have a general manager with that knowledge. You know the value of training and you have the ability to plan three to five years ahead.

America's Powersports falls into the above range, meaning it is operating very efficiently. They are helping set the bar for operational efficiency in the industry.

OK, suppose you employ 3 people per million in sales. Does that mean you're less efficient or a poor manager of people? That depends on a few other factors. If you are ramping up and aggressively attempting to grow your business you might be overstaffed for the short-term but properly staffed if the incremental goal you've set is attainable.

One thing is clear: the consolidators are setting the standard for the industry in terms of efficiency.

Consolidation is also bringing about changes elsewhere in the industry. An inhibitor to faster consolidation appears to be related, at least in part, to the computer systems needed to generate the appropriate reports for management. The major DMS providers have been working to address that problem. In the past a dealer with say, 25 computer terminals was considered very large. Now, consolidators have the need for literally hundreds of terminals and a way to connect a great many stores together. These systems are large and relative to those in the average independent dealership, expensive. They also require very well trained operations personnel.

The dealer management software providers have been challenged to come up with solutions for these large, high volumes, multi-store operations – another shift in the business.

I believe that the consolidators, using what's called "best practices" and consolidated purchasing have already shown they can generate higher profit margins than the average independent store.

Consider what an advantage it would be if you were to place orders with aftermarket suppliers in huge quantities that would assure the best possible prices. Could you expect to negotiate preferential treatment or better prices if you could assure the distributor that your purchases would be in the tens of millions of dollars annually? I think so.

Of course, only time will tell. As our economy continues its roller coaster antics we may, finally, see an impact on our industry. However, I do believe that these major consolidators are pragmatic strategic thinkers and have already taken the possible economic changes into consideration.

We already know the advantages warehouse distributor consolidation has brought. It's meant fewer backorders and faster delivery from regional warehouses. On the OEM side, Kawasaki and Suzuki claim they will benefit from more in-house creative talent and consolidation of component purchase orders.

Chapter 36

THE NEW COMPETITION

We've seen it in almost every industry including ours – diversification. We've also seen consolidation. Yet we continue to grow albeit at a more modest pace than in past years.

Now, however, we have new challenges that require us to rethink our marketing and rethink our need to diversify. What are these challenges? New competition in the form of non-traditional product lines and non-traditional retail threats.

There are now more products from both Asia and Europe. There is also more temptation to experiment with diverse lines in an attempt to continue to grow. Is diversification into non-traditional product lines a reasonable option?

Pep Boys has diversified into our market by offering small displacement scooters, ATVs and mini-dirt bikes through their 600+ stores. That move is causing considerable angst in our industry. But what about our diversifying further into the lawn and garden market as witnessed by many lawn care products being offered at the Powersports Dealer Expo show in Indy in recent years? Could that be causing similar angst on their side? After all, we have large and very well equipped service departments – often larger and better equipped than those who sell lawn and garden products.

Today's reality is that the powersports business is made up of mostly independent entrepreneurs who sell what they enjoy or feel will fit into their marketplace.

Most other industries market through chain retailers whose stores are large, cookie cutter outlets. Non-enthusiasts staff most big box stores.

We can change our displays, brands and marketing strategies virtually overnight. The chain stores don't have that option; they must abide by corporate decisions. Chain store managers know that personal opinions, likes and dislikes don't count when it comes to inventory selection.

Where are we most vulnerable? In the entry level and the youth dirt bike and ATV markets. Why are we more vulnerable in those markets? They have lower gross profit margins and produce fewer bottom line dollars. Therefore, we spend less time focusing on them. In our industry opinions, likes, dislikes, and marketing focus do count.

The independent retailers in the lawn and garden business are more like us when it comes to opinions, likes and dislikes. These independent dealers spend less time on the low-end power mowers because the big boxes like Wal-Mart, K-Mart, Target, Sears, Lowe's and Home Depot buy these inexpensive units by the truckload and often sell at a very small profit to build store traffic. That makes it all but impossible for the independent dealer to compete with the big boxes that target the first-time buyer.

Now many more big boxes are beginning to sell these small dirt bikes and ATVs that don't need to be registered. The same first time lawnmower buyer may also be a first time youth dirt bike or ATV buyer.

Our big box competitors may appear formidable but can be less so if your dealership rethinks the youth market. Where do they falter? They miss the mark on training, service and activity venues. They don't have the personnel or the time to guide their customer. You do. They don't know where the closed courses or powersports parks are located. They don't have trained sales people who can properly instruct the new buyer on how to use this newly purchased unit. They won't have the apparel that goes with the unit nor the understanding needed to suggest what apparel is appropriate and why. You possess all these skills.

Someone who purchases an under-$400 mini-dirt bike or a $900 ATV from a big box may not know that purchase is just the beginning. Boots, helmet, body armor, trailers, etc. almost make the cheap dirt bike a loss leader. You know what it takes and it's up to you to inform and educate both the youth and his or her parents.

You not only know where the events are but also can suggest the new buyer attend to get a feel of what it's like before they decide to let their youngster become a competitive rider. To take it one step further, one dealer told me he was going to buy a Pep Boys mini-dirt bike and an ATV so he could show the customer the difference between what he had to offer and what Pep Boys was selling. He felt confident that he could show the potential buyer why what he was selling was worth the difference and then some.

The advantage goes to you if you focus on service, relationship marketing and activity. I know of many dealers who send a company truck to these youth events with spare parts and enough tools and trained people to take care of most minor accident or "fall down" problems. Those with whom I've spoken say it has been well worth the effort.

There are some people who just won't buy from you for a myriad of reasons; the biggest being price. Then there are those who believe you don't care. There's not much you can do when it comes to someone who focuses on price alone. But you can do something for those who think you don't care. Caring is the first step in developing a long term or on-going relationship. That's the business you're in: relationships.

Chapter 37

E-POWER

The power of "E" is not the e-commerce we hear so much about, but email. Currently, tens if not hundreds of millions of Americans have at least one email address. Research indicates that those with email addressees check their electronic mail much more often than they visit their post office or make the trip to their mailbox. Therein lies a wonderful opportunity for communications, advertising and building a loyal and long-term customer base.

Before I start I must give credit to someone who gave me the input that became the genesis of this article. Unfortunately, I don't have the person's name. He was a participant in the audience of a seminar I conducted at a Harley-Davidson new model introduction a few years ago. The subject of my seminar was "Disruptive Technology." The focus related to the Internet and how this emerging technology is changing the way we do business, gather information, do research, buy, sell and communicate with each other.

During the question and answer portion of the program this Harley-Davidson dealer offered a suggestion that was great. He said that there's a line on every form he uses that requests the customer's email address. He went on to say that he considers a customer's email address as important as his or her phone number and perhaps even more important than their physical address.

Think about it. Having your Web site and waiting for visitors is like fishing and waiting for a fish to bite. Sending out email is like gathering all the fish together before you put your baited hook in the water.

Using email is cheaper than buying ads in the newspaper. It's quicker and more personal too.

Some people say that spam has killed email – that it's dead. The numbers say otherwise. A recent study in late 2004 showed that 90 percent of B-to-C (business to consumer) marketers are using some form of email marketing or e-newsletters. Sixty percent of those planned to increase their usage even more. Email is definitely not dead.

As of this writing in late 2004, it is a necessary part of retail marketing today. Why? Because so many more consumers are online and communicate that way.

However, with the passage of the CAN-Spam Act in the United States in late 2003, email marketing has become trickier. You now have to comply with certain requirements for any commercial email you send. Those requirements are not difficult to comply with, but they do require that you have a clear understanding of them, that you provide "opt out" capabilities, and that your email records be well organized.

That's why if you are going to use email for marketing purposes I strongly recommend that you first familiarize yourself with this law. Because laws change from time to time I won't attempt to discuss the requirements here.

EMAIL MARKETING SOFTWARE SERVICES

I also strongly recommend you sign up for one of the commercial email marketing software services on the Web. Such services manage customer email opt-in and opt-out preferences automatically. These services are reasonably priced; a decent one costs as little as $25 a month. They will manage all your customers' email addresses and other contact information. They can handle all aspects of your email marketing program – from soup to nuts.

Some of these services are very sophisticated and can track your customers' preferences as to riding type, preferred brands and apparel styles, interests, etc. They'll even personalize email messages with the click of your mouse. You can send out hundreds or thousands of messages addressing each customer on a first name basis, in a matter of minutes.

These programs contain ready-made templates that you can use to compose e-newsletters and other messages. All you need to do is drop in some digital images and type out your message.

The better ones maintain "whitelist" status. That means email marketing messages sent out through their systems will not be blocked by the major ISPs like AOL.

The email services help you market effectively at the same time as they help you comply with the CAN-Spam Act, because they organize your records. They manage the entire subscription process seamlessly. If a customer opts out of mailings, the system deletes his email address. The better systems even prevent the email address from being re-entered inadvertently.

An entire book could be written on email marketing alone. I will attempt only to hit the high points here. Following are some ways that a dealer can use this tool to make his life better, improve the customer's experience, increase customer loyalty, improve the dealership's CSI and, finally, produce more profit while reducing costs. OK, so I'm a dreamer, but maybe not. Read on. Consider using email – "push technology" – department by department.

SERVICE DEPARTMENT

Instead of phoning the customer when his bike is ready to be picked up and talking to some kid who may or may not get the message across, why not notify them via email? You could include a note that may have such information as the total price, suggestions for further service and information about events such as an open house or an organized ride.

If you have to give a customer bad news, for example, the part needed to complete the repair is on backorder, you could pass that message on along with an anticipated arrival date and ask the customer to continue to check his email because now, you can keep them updated and informed. It has been found that using this form of communication is less likely to cause an emotional response than giving the bad news in person or on the phone. If the customer is angered by the information they are forced to write down their response. That action causes them to think about the situation, thereby reducing the angst.

PARTS DEPARTMENT

Now you can notify the customer that the special part or accessory they ordered has arrived. If the order is not complete you can advise them of that too. It's always better to be as fast with the bad news as with the good news. And, like the above example, it is less likely to elicit an emotional response.

If you know of some customers who are always interested in the newest and latest thing, wouldn't it be nice to send them an email telling them about that new item you just got in? How about taking a digital picture of the new item and including it in your email along with information to help them decide if they'd like to come in to see the accessory or part in person?

APPAREL DEPARTMENT

As in the service and parts departments, you can now notify the customer that the jacket they ordered has arrived. Then invite them to come in and try it on to make sure it's exactly what they want.

The digital camera can be a great aid here too. For example, you receive some new styles. If you feel your female customers might be interested, you could take a few pictures of a staff member modeling the garment and send it to your female customers who have requested product information be sent from time to time. Obviously, the same could be done for guys interested in the latest men's styles of riding apparel.

Unit Sales Department

OK, we've talked about that special order situation in the service, parts and apparel department. The same applies here in unit sales.

I know that most dealers have customers looking for specific models of used units too. What better way to notify a customer that you may have just what they're looking for and even have a few photos of the unit you could email to them.

If you sponsor events, it would be interesting to take digital photos and email them to the participants along with a note that you'd be glad to print them a photo quality copy of the emailed version. That, I could assure you, will bring them to your door.

Collecting Email Addresses

So how do you collect customer email addresses and start building up this valuable list? Ask for them!

So here's what I suggest you do today! Put a pad on the counter and ask every customer to print his or her name and email address on the pad. Tell them how you're going to stay in touch with them via email.

Change any of your computer-based forms to include a line that requires the customer to list his or her email address. If you plan to order more forms I urge you to increase the address field to include a blank line for the customer's email address.

Give reasons on your Web site for visitors to provide their email addresses. Perhaps offer a free T-shirt drawing, or a free e-newsletter that you send out once a month. Include an e-newsletter sign-up box prominently on the home page and on every single page of your site.

Before you know it, you will have a large – and valuable – customer email list.

Chapter 38

GO WEST, THEY SAID

I'm old enough to remember when the Japanese bikes were first imported to the USA. Honda was the first. They focused on exporting 50cc to 90cc displacement bikes. Getting a franchise was both easy and (by today's standards) extremely inexpensive.

Dealers soon clamored for larger displacement bikes. Soon they were selling Japanese-made 250cc parallel twins, followed by 305cc then a DOHC 450cc twin. Yamaha entered the market with 2-stroke bikes but soon produced a 650cc parallel twin. (I owned one). Omega brought in a 650cc twin. Later the name was changed to Kawasaki. In those early days Suzuki exported 2-stroke bikes only.

The reputation of Japanese bikes was less than sterling. As time passed the perception of quality changed. The English twins were now saddled with less than sterling service reputations. It wasn't long before the German, American and Japanese bikes took over the market.

Fast-forward about 40 years. Units produced in Japan have become the envy of most when it comes to reliability and quality; not only motorcycles but in cars as well. However, with the increase in quality came a substantial increase in cost.

Japan was fast becoming a major exporter of superior products. That meant the Japanese OEMs needed to employ more engineers and other highly trained and, therefore, better paid workers. As wages climbed so did the prices of the products.

Now that labor costs in Japan are very close to labor costs in the USA the price of their offerings of both cars and motorcycles is very close to those made here or in Europe. According to JD Powers, the quality, fit and finish of Japanese motorcycles and cars is superior to ours. JD Powers also report that customer satisfaction scores are higher for Japanese cars, trucks and motorcycles than are those made here or in Europe.

To remain competitive every manufacturer both here and abroad must find ways to reduce costs while improving fit, finish and overall quality. Enter outsourcing ... enter China.

The Japanese manufacturers got there first. According to a report I received from China recently, Honda, Yamaha and Suzuki now have "International Partnerships" with Chinese manufacturers. These manufacturing partners have the capacity to produce 630,000 units per month.

As of this writing most are small displacement engine units like those sold to Pep Boys. However, many of these same companies are applying for certification to comply with the EPA and DOT in order to export here for sale and use on our highways. In order to get that certification they must meet some rather stringent requirements. They must also set up distribution channels.

Until very recently, China did not abide by international patents or copyrights. However, since the Chinese government owns a part of every Chinese manufacturer and is looking at export as a way to grow their economy, they are beginning to change the rules. Unlike our government China brooks very little interference or input with their policies. When they say change, manufacturers fall in step.

How big is China's motorcycle and ATV export market? Huge. For now they are focusing on other third-world countries that have few import restrictions like those imposed by the EPA and DOT. I say for now because the competition among the 155 motorcycle and ATV makers in China has gotten so fierce that profits have all but disappeared.

The Chinese companies that are partnered with Japanese OEMs are among the strongest and most capable of the more than 150 manufacturers. Many have been making parts for their Japanese partners for decades. Keep in mind that China produces a whopping 9,000,000 motorcycles per year.

Wuyang, a Chinese producer, has recently entered into an international partnership with an Italian company and will soon be exporting 180cc engines to use in their bikes. I've heard that several other Italian makers are also looking to supply China with engines for scooters and motorcycles. Meanwhile, both Japan and Korea are exporting designs and technology to China. Eighteen of the largest Chinese motorcycle manufacturers are making huge investments in research and development.

What about prices? The stated FOB prices range is from $300 to about $600 for four-stroke bikes with engines up to 150cc.

What's coming next? Loncin, a high-tech Chinese company, has created an unusual engine. It is a 400cc, fuel injected twin. The engine is made of "advanced ceramic material," rather than cast aluminum. It's my understanding that the ceramic materials are less affected by temperature changes.

The major OEMs are investing up to a whopping 20 percent of sales in research and development. It's amazing what a company can accomplish if they don't have to deal with things like insurance, unions, paying a living wage and government interference. How much could be accomplished here if workers were paid an average of 61 cents per hour?

To sum up: I believe we are going to see a replay of 40 odd years ago. This time the new emerging industrial giant is China. They are not space limited like Japan. They have a huge work force willing to work for very low wages and in a relatively primitive environment.

How soon will it happen? It's happening right now. How fast will it grow? I predict about 10 to 20 percent growth per year.

Will they start producing larger displacement engines? A Korean company currently produces a 650cc DOHC V-twin that is being imported now. Many Chinese companies are just waiting for approval to ramp up manufacturing of their large displacement engines. Depending on their success, others will follow.

What about distribution? According to the MIC, there are over 6,000 franchised motorcycle outlets in the USA now and more than 7,000 non-franchised outlets. That means these Chinese companies will have great potential.

What are the inhibitors? China does not fully understand the way America does business. They must learn how to deal with our governmental agencies and to honor patents and copyrights. They will need to develop a supporting infrastructure, hire qualified people and make a substantial investment here in the USA.

Look through the pages of any current powersports trade magazines and you'll see slick full-page, four-color ads offering scooters, ATVs and motorcycles from some of the more prestigious Chinese makers. The reality is that China will soon be a major player in supplying motorcycles and ATVs to the United States. We'd best learn how to deal with it.

Chapter 39

THE POWER OF 20

Over the past few years I've been invited to participate in several conference calls with Bill Shenk's Powerhouse Dealer Services 20 club members. It was quite an honor to sit in by phone and just listen to what concerns dealers had and were willing to share. Oh yeah, at the end of the call I was able to put in my "two-cents' worth."

There are many such 20 clubs run by a wide variety of facilitators. Unfortunately, only a small percentage of dealers are participating members. The value of these 20 groups to a dealer's quality of life and bottom line cannot be overstressed. Here's what I discovered.

First, the dealers with whom I participated in these calls seemed to know and truly like each other. They were great communicators and welcomed constructive criticism. They shared ideas and had some very imaginative and creative solutions and suggestions on ways to make their operations run more smoothly. They were willing to share their concerns and even discuss their individual problems with specific staff members. They also shared their need to learn how to be better managers.

Rather than the one-upmanship I've witnessed in different settings these dealers related to each other more like members of the same team. Bill Shenk had the dealers' numbers and using some special software he has created was able to tell them how they were doing, where they were strong and what they need to address to continue to be profitable and grow.

I have some dealer friends who are extremely bright people and run very profitable operations. However, not very many belong to 20 clubs. They really don't know what they're missing both in management training skills and more importantly the fact that they are leaving too much money on the table.

If there is one area where our industry needs help it's training. The OEMs do a good job at offering training for technicians. The major DMS providers do a good job of training dealers and department managers on how to use their computer systems to track and monitor their dealerships. A few of the OEMs offer additional training for a variety of department managers. Some offer special classes for owners as well.

We have come a long way since I started in the industry more than 40 years ago. We still have a long way to go as the business shows signs of "maturity."

Today, most dealers fully understand the principle of expansion but not as many understand the dynamics of contraction. The latter is more painful and requires different skill sets. The best way I know of to hone one's skills for both these conditions is by getting involved with like minded dealers in different parts of the country and sharing their thoughts in a (more or less) structured environment.

There seems to be a universal opinion regarding sharing information with OEMs. Historically, I can understand why. In too many cases the information was turned around and used against the dealers who had provided it. I don't know of any instances of this happening in the past decade or so but dealers have very long memories.

The problem is if dealers are not willing to share their information with anyone then how can they learn? The simple answer is they will learn by making mistakes. That too often means losing money. Then trying something else, which may work or may lose still more money. It's a hit or miss proposition at best.

So, with whom can a dealer confidently share sensitive information? The simple answer is with their fellow dealers, most of whom have the same issues and concerns. I know of no better way to find out that what you thought was a good idea had been tried repeatedly and failed. Now, you don't have to go through the time, expense and angst in a futile attempt to do something doomed to failure.

Probably the greatest benefit of the 20 clubs is dealers telling each other what they've done that worked, as well as things they've done that didn't. They can do this in a non-threatening setting knowing that their information will stay within the group.

Over the years I've been reluctant to recommend dealers join any one specific group although I have suggested they get involved with at least one. Some of the OEMs have created such clubs, however, many dealers are reluctant to share information at that level for the reasons I've listed above.

A few of the DMS providers have created similar groups but that's not their core business. In the past they haven't given it sufficient focus and attention to offer the value today's dealers insist upon. Perhaps that will change.

I've been told of some 20 clubs focusing almost exclusively on F&I and used bikes. Others just look at the numbers. The fact is, no matter what their specialty they are all beneficial based on the reality that the dealers have an opportunity to sit down and talk to each other about things that really matter.

My advice? Find a 20 club whose facilitator and members you can feel comfortable with, and join it today.

Chapter 40

USED VS. NEW

There are more than 3,000 used motorcycles for sale on eBay. Next month there will be 3,000 more. There are some real bargains, some collectables, some rare bikes, quite a few custom creations and many uncommon or no-longer-in-existence brands. One thing most have in common, however, is good condition, low mileage and a low price.

For example, there's a new looking 2002 Honda 1800cc VTX with fewer than 4,000 miles on the odometer that sold for $8,700. A 2001Honda CBR 600 F4I with 700 on the clock, sold for $5,700. There are 725 more Hondas on that same site, many of which are being offered by dealers who will take care of crating and shipping for a reasonable fee.

Would you like an almost new 1999 Yamaha Road Star driven less than 3,000 miles for $7,975? That's what it sold for. Or how about a 2001 V-Star 1100 Custom that has been ridden only 390 miles for $6,500? You can get a 2003 Buell Firebolt XB9R ridden less than 1,000 miles for about $6,000. A 2001 Buell Blast with less than 135 miles on the clock recently sold for $1,699. A 1998 Suzuki GSXR 750 Race Bike GSX-R sold for $3,000.

OK, so you get the point. What this means is that there is a real glut of used bikes on the market. Add to that the fact that 75 percent of all bikes sold are not sold by franchised dealers but by one individual to another. Yes, our market has and continues to change. Today's rider is past 40 years of age and as a rule , keeps his or her motorcycle in better condition and rides fewer miles than a decade ago.

Are these used bikes being sold on the Internet worthy of consideration to someone interested in getting into the sport? I think so, considering that most are not only well kept but many are liquid-cooled touring bikes that have not been overstressed or ridden hard. Besides, water-cooled bikes don't wear out as quickly as those that are air-cooled. So, what's happening? Zero percent financing is a lure that makes it easier for the experienced rider to get a new bike. An unstable economy aids by creating a disorderly marketplace. And bikes just a few years old look almost exactly the same as the latest iteration of that same bike.

What does this mean to you if you're a franchise holder looking to sell new bikes? What does it mean to the OEM who has no interest in selling used bikes but wants to make sure you have plenty of new ones on the floor? It means crunch time!

It probably means that you may be paying too much for used bikes and that perhaps market pricing should be considered instead of the published used bike evaluations.

Entry level is "used." I know there are some who will argue that point but these are the same people who started their riding experience on someone else's bike or on a used one they bought. If the new rider isn't sure he or she will really like motorcycling it's safer to buy a lower cost used bike where the depreciation has already been taken by the first owner, than to buy a new one and then discover it's not what they really wanted. Besides, if the new biker has an older bike other bikers are less likely to think he's a beginner nerd.

That "new biker" bad vibe has even affected the apparel market. Some motorcycle leathers come pre-scuffed and look like they've been around for a while, making the owner look more like he's an experienced rider. In our ego driven environment, that's a good thing.

The economy, the Baby Boomers moving on and our slowness in answering new market demands could be hurting us in the long term. We need to avoid that by realizing that ***used*** outsells ***new*** three to one. That ***used*** can be as profitable – or more – than ***new*** and that most consumers would rather buy from a dealer than from an individual.

Your OEM won't be very comfortable with you focusing much attention on showing and selling competitive used bikes but I believe that doing so is a long range growth strategy that will allow you to increase you market share and continue to grow despite any shifts in the economy.

Some more aggressive dealers look for ways to buy, refurbish and resell used bikes. By the way, "previously owned" is fast replacing the word "used."

Many non-franchised dealers make a very good living selling tricked out used bikes. Some other dealers, unfortunately, avoid offering used bikes altogether or will only offer a used bike if it's the same brand that they sell as new.

The motorcycle business is unlike the car business in many aspects. The main difference is that cars are "needs" whereas the majority of motorcycles are purchased as "wants."

However, we could well emulate at least one of the car dealers' marketing strategies. Most car dealers have large inventories of used vehicles. Many go to the wholesale auctions to buy brands other than what they sell as new. The reason is that if the customer comes onto their lot they've won the first round, no matter what brand that customer came in to see. From then on it's how the salesperson interacts with the customer that may end in a sale. How professional that salesperson is and how helpful, may well determine if the consumer will return in the future or if he or she could become a loyal customer.

Remember, too, that the average car dealer derives about six percent of his net profits from selling new cars. The rest comes from F&I, used car sales and service.

FINAL THOUGHTS

The retail powersports and accessory business is much more challenging, interesting and romantic than most other professions or jobs. The frustration experienced by many retail powersports dealers and employees, I believe, is created by lack of direction and training combined with less than positive attitudes.

One of my favorite lines is: the three most important qualities of character are attitude, attitude and attitude, but not necessarily in that order. Attitude is the first thing to which a customer responds.

Dealers are constantly meeting new people. If the dealer has an attitude that conveys the impression he's glad to see the customer and enjoys life, the experience and the business will be more satisfying. Maintaining a positive attitude has become more difficult as business grows more complex. Your attitude can and does, make a difference in your business. Attitude is what turns people "on" or "off."

Business is not as formidable as some think. All the rules are written down. You must learn and follow those rules. Success, in business, is measured in green.

What I have attempted to do in this book is to use my training and experience combined with information from literally hundreds of dealers I've met over the years to address concerns which I feel are paramount to most dealers.

Now it's time for you to go on to greater success.

- John Wyckoff